Frank Mouritz
The Influence of Econ n
US-China Relations

INTERNATIONAL AND SECURITY STUDIES

Book series edited by
Prof. Dr. Sven Bernhard Gareis
&
Prof. Dr. Johannes Varwick
/
herausgegeben von
Prof. Dr. Sven Bernhard Gareis
&
Prof. Dr. Johannes Varwick

Volume/Band 9

Frank Mouritz

The Influence of Economic Interdependence on US-China Relations

An Analysis of Economic Incentives for
Continued Cooperation

Verlag Barbara Budrich
Opladen • Berlin • Toronto 2021

A CIP catalogue record for this book is available from
Die Deutsche Bibliothek (The German Library)

© 2021   by Barbara Budrich Publishers, Opladen, Berlin & Toronto
www.budrich.eu

ISBN   978-3-8474-2516-8 (Paperback)
eISBN   978-3-8474-1684-5 (eBook)
DOI   10.3224/84742516

Das Werk einschließlich aller seiner Teile ist urheberrechtlich geschützt. Jede Verwertung außerhalb der engen Grenzen des Urheberrechtsgesetzes ist ohne Zustimmung des Verlages unzulässig und strafbar. Das gilt insbesondere für Vervielfältigungen, Übersetzungen, Mikroverfilmungen und die Einspeicherung und Verarbeitung in elektronischen Systemen.

Die Deutsche Bibliothek – CIP-Einheitsaufnahme
Ein Titeldatensatz für die Publikation ist bei der Deutschen Bibliothek erhältlich.

Verlag Barbara Budrich Barbara Budrich Publishers
Stauffenbergstr. 7. D-51379 Leverkusen Opladen, Germany
86 Delma Drive. Toronto, ON M8W 4P6 Canada
www.budrich.eu

Jacket illustration/Umschlaggestaltung: Bettina Lehfeldt, Kleinmachnow, Germany – www.lehfeldtgraphic.de
Technical Editing/Typographisches Lektorat: Anja Borkam, Jena, Germany – kontakt@lektorat-borkam.de
Printed by/Druck: Books on Demand GmbH, Norderstedt, Germany
Printed in Europe

Table of Contents

Preface

This book project was started before Donald Trump was elected as US president in 2016 and subsequently started to take measures to alter economic relations with China. The trade tariffs and other non-tariff measures that both the US and China have enacted from 2017 onwards have distorted bilateral economic interaction to such an extent that trade data after 2016 is not giving a realistic picture of how strong the economic interdependencies between the US and China actually are. Thus, this book only uses data up to 2016 and in some exceptions 2017. The added value of looking at 2016 and earlier is that the results of this book can serve as "baseline" for how the economic interdependencies looked like without manipulation. Obviously, this baseline will never be fully restored because trade ties are constantly changing - even without trade disputes - but it gives the best overview of how much both sides benefit from economic interaction and how much both sides stand to lose. A discussion on the effect of economic interdependence only makes sense in reference to this baseline.

While the US-China trade dispute changed bilateral trade relations, it did not end economic interdependence nor was economic interdependence irrelevant for the dispute. On the contrary, how far either side wanted to go was very much influenced by economic interdependencies and by how high the economic costs for effected industries and consumers would be. The US started with targeted tariffs for sectors that are less dependent on imports from China and only slowly expanded tariffs to more dependent sectors, while at the same time a vast catalogue of exceptions was introduced in an attempt to reduce the negative effects to the US economy. Measures that would directly hurt US consumers like tariffs on consumer electronics were postponed several times and, in the end, never went into effect. Likewise, the Chinese side tried to hurt its own economy as little as possible and targeted those sectors of the US economy with counter-tariffs that are especially vulnerable to a cut-off of trade ties. This behaviour shows that both sides have an interest not to escalate the dispute and that economic interdependence gives an incentive to continue cooperation even during times of tensions.

Some political commentators and academics see the US-China trade dispute as an example of "weaponised interdependence", where the US tries to use China's dependence on exports to the US as a pressure point to extort concessions from China. Applying the concept of "weaponised interdependence" on US-China relations is not appropriate because it describes a constellation in which a country can use his structural advantages in an asymmetrical network to coerce other countries. US-China trade relations are not asymmetrical but are characterised by a high degree of mutual dependence as this book will show. Even talking about asymmetry within interdependencies does not seem logical because for countries to be interdependent means that both sides are more or less equally dependent on each other. The results of this book proof that that the US economy depends about as much on the Chinese economy as the other way around which is why a "weaponization" of interdependence necessarily causes harm to both sides and is not an effective leverage to extort concessions.

The so called „Phase One Trade Deal", which was signed by the US and China in January 2020, was portrayed by the Trump administration as great breakthrough, but it does not contain any major concessions from the Chinese side and a majority of US economists agree that it does not make up for the costs of the trade dispute. The content of the trade deal is not discussed in this book because it was finalised in the fall of 2019, but the detailed analysis of economic interdependencies across economic sectors and across trade flows in this book is the perfect basis to put the content and details of the deal into perspective. The deal contains chapters regarding intellectual property, technology transfer and financial services that are meant to make it easier (and fairer) for US companies to do business with and in China, but many of the clauses are only declarations of intendent so it remains to be seen if and how China will implement these promises. The more substantial part of the agreement is a commitment by the Chinese government to increase imports from the United States. China promises to import US goods worth 63,9 billion US dollars in 2020 and 98,2 billion US dollars in 2021 on top of what it imported from the United States in 2017.

The deal also defines how much of which product categories China shall import. Manufactured goods make up the largest share with intended imports of additional 32,9 billion US dollars on top of the 2017 baseline in 2020 and 44,8 billion US dollars in 2021. Annex 6.1. explicitly lists electrical equipment, machinery, aircraft, medical devises, and microchips as products belonging to manufactured goods. As described in chapter 4.4.2. of this book these are exactly the types of goods that China wants to buy from the United States anyway because it has no sufficient domestic production and because there are no sufficient alternative suppliers to cover all of China's vast demand for these goods. The same is true for the agricultural goods like soybeans. China cut most of its soybean imports from the US during the height of the trade dispute and instead bought more soybeans from Brazil which were more expensive. In addition, China even had to substitute soybeans with more expensive feedstuff because other suppliers were not able to increase soybean cultivation fast enough. Thus, China is more than happy to resume soybean imports from the US.

While China has an interest in buying US goods, the volume of 63,9 billion US dollars of additional imports on top of the 2017 baseline in 2020 and 98,2 billion US dollars in 2021 seems ambitious given that China imported 129,9 billion US dollars of US goods in 2017. China would need to import roughly 50% more from the US in 2020 than in 2017 and another 23% more in 2021. In order to reach these goals China would most certainly need cut imports from other countries and buy US products instead (e.g. buy airplanes from Boeing instead of Airbus). Therefore, the trade deal could turn out to be very disadvantageous for China's other major trading partners.

Even if China fulfils all purchase commitments then the amount is still not nearly enough to close the deficit in the United States' trade balance with China, which amounted to 375,5 billion US dollars in 2017, nor is the deal taking into consideration that what has really pushed the deficit over the last years is the expansion of Chinese exports to the United States. If China's exports continue to grow with a similar speed - simply because of US demand - then the deficit will even further increase despite higher Chinese imports of US goods. This is especially true if the Phase One Trade Deal is not followed up by another deal that will cover expanding Chinese purchases beyond 2021.

So far, the trade deal did not work. The US trade deficit with China in July 2020 is 4,36% wider than four years ago in July 2016 when Donald Trump was on the campaign trail and promised to bring down the US trade deficit by being tough on China and the EU. The overall US trade deficit with the rest of the world even reached its highest level in 12 years in July 2020. (Whether the trade balance is a good economic indicator to assess the value of economic interaction and if the United States should actively try to reduce the deficit with China is discussed extensively in chapter 4.3.3.).

1 Introduction

1.1 Addressing a Research Gap in the Empirical Study of Economic Interdependence

Research on economic interdependence is heavily dominated by quantitative methods and almost exclusively executed by Anglo-American researchers. Consequently, this field of study has seen no real innovation in the last years. Current research on the topic mainly consists of studies which analyse the correlation between economic exchange and political conflict. They differ from each other primarily by the selection of data sets and application of different mathematic methods. Remarkably, the findings often contradict each other, creating the impression that results depend to a large extent on the chosen methods and personal interpretation.

The stagnation in this field of research could be addressed by conducting more qualitative studies. Ripsman and Blanchard argue that qualitative research would open up new perspectives and generate deeper insights into the effects of economic interdependence (Ripsman and Blanchard 2003). This study wants to address the lack of qualitative research by conducting a qualitative case study on the effect of economic interdependence on bilateral relations between two states. A bilateral scenario was chosen because it allows analysing interdependence in a limited setting and focuses on the actor level rather than the systemic level. After all, states are still the key players when it comes to hard power in the international system. Due to their level of economic interconnectedness the most suitable research subjects for such a study are the US and China, which are arguably the most interdependent countries at present.

What make this country pair even more suitable for this study is the importance of US-China relations for international politics in the 21st century. The way the US, the current superpower, and China, an emerging superpower, handle their relationship will decide about the future world order. Due to differences in the form of government, organisation of the economy, culture, and society the relationship bears significant potential for confrontation. Furthermore, China and the US often take opposite views on foreign policy matters and compete for influence in international organisations (Buzan 2004, 71 & 142). This makes bilateral relations a tender subject. However, despite these differences, economic relations remain strong and vital for the economic performance of both countries. This constellation makes the country pair very interesting for research on the interaction of economic and political relations. Therefore, US-China relations are a well-suited case to examine the effect of economic interdependence on political relations.

1.2 US-China Relations in the Academic Debate

Events in recent years have made it obvious that the political world order is in transition. Emerging major economies like Brazil, Russia, India, China, and South Africa (BRICS) have challenged "Western" authority and US hegemony over global affairs. For a time, it looked like the world would move from a US-centric, unipolar post-Cold War order to a multipolar one. However, in the aftermath of the 2007-2009 financial crisis the BRICS have lost economic momentum. Only China was able keep up high economic growth rates, although on a lower level than before the financial crisis. The US also experienced difficult economic times but was able to stabilise gradually (World Bank 2016). This development has led to a situation in which China remains the sole serious competitor to continued US hegemony. Thus, world politics in the 21st century will be deeply shaped by the nature of the Sino-American relationship. For the future development of world affairs it will be crucial whether the relationship will be characterised by conflict or cooperation; or in the words of Henry Kissinger "rivalry or partnership" (Kissinger 2014, 227).

One group of scholars, prominently represented by the realist scholar John J. Mearsheimer, sees China as a "potential peer competitor" to the US and expects a return of 19-century-style "great-power politics" in case China's economic development continues (Mearsheimer 2001, 360; 2010, 381–96), because "a wealthy China would not be a status quo power but an aggressive state determined to achieve regional hegemony" (Mearsheimer 2001, 402). It is worth noting that Mearsheimer already made this prediction in 2001 at a time when China was still far away from being a serious competitor to US hegemony. The main argument of this group of scholars is rooted in power transition theory, which postulates that rising powers will inevitably come into conflict with established powers over the political structure and rules of the international system. Power transition theory assumes that it is in the interest of a rising power to revise the status quo for its own benefits and that it will do so once it is strong enough. Contrarily, the established power has an interest in preserving the status quo as it participated in designing the current international political order and benefits from the existing set of rules (Organski and Kugler 1980; Organski 1968).

In a constellation where the rising power is close to reach power equilibrium, which some argue is already the case for the US and China, both powers are fraught with uncertainty about their competitor's behaviour. According to power transition theory, the rising power must fear that the established power will try to stop its rise as long as it is still superior and the established power must fear that the rising power will try to dictate its own set of rules once power has shifted. The uncertainty about the intentions of the competitor can ultimately lead to a security dilemma, pre-emptive actions and possibly even trigger a military confrontation. Therefore, periods of power transition are referred to as "zones of contention and probable war" by advocates of power transition theory (Tammen, Kugler, and Lemke 2000).

In a large-scale historic case file project for the Harvad Belfer Center Graham Allison and his team have identified 16 cases of power transition between a dominant hegemon and a major rising power in the last 500 years of which 12 resulted in a war over hegemonic power. Presumably the most prominent one is the case of Wilhelminian Germany challenging British hegemony at the beginning of the 20th century which ultimately resulted in World War One. The large number of wars during times of shifting power support power transition theory, though Allison's case study also shows that more recent power shifts have been less conflictual. Only three out of seven power shifts in the 20th century resulted in war (Allison 2015).

Mearsheimer and his fellows view China in the classic role of a rising power, unsatisfied with the current world order and striving for a revision on its own terms. In fact, the USA and China favour significantly different concepts of world order. While the US traditionally advocate a system of pooled sovereignty and extensive networks of international legal and organisational structures, China takes a stand for bilateral problem solving and absolute national sovereignty as a shield against foreign interference. Opposing views on democracy and human rights constitute further sources for disagreement and conflict (Kissinger 2014, 6–8 & 229–30). Because of its non-conformance with "Western" values and its "alienation from the dominant international society" Barry Buzan calls China "the most obvious challenger [to the US and its global hegemony]" (Buzan 2004, 71 & 142).

While China surely is at odds with many aspects of the still predominant liberal-democratic world order, it has at the same time greatly benefitted from this system. China's rise was based on economic liberalisation and gradual integration into the world society. In order to achieve economic development it was necessary for China to adapt to capitalist market principles and to play by international rules (Ikenberry 2008, 30–34). This pragmatic approach to political and economic realities speaks against the thesis of China being a revisionist state.

Academics and politicians who believe that China will continue political liberalisation and engage in more global cooperation point to China's self-imposed foreign policy strategy of a "peaceful rise" through "peaceful development", which emphasises a peaceful coexistence between great powers. They argue that the US engagement policy, which was started by Henry Kissinger in 1969, has already significantly changed China and they expect that China will continue to gradually adjust to values and structures of the international system if the US is willing to share power and accepts China as an important and responsible stakeholder in the current world order (Ikenberry 2008; Bijian 2005; Zoellick 2005).

This integrative approach towards China is criticised as "sleeping with the (potential) enemy" (Papayoanou and Kastner 2000). Sceptics claim that the "peaceful development" rhetoric is a Chinese scheme to hide its brightness and bide its time; just as a rising power would do according to power transition theory. They see China's offer to establish a "new type of great power relations", one that is designed to avoid historic mistakes, as a way to reintroduce spheres of influence and obtain regional hegemony over East Asia (Glosserman 2013; Erickson and Liff 2014; White, Weihua, and Jianmin 2014). Furthermore, it is argued that even if the current Chinese leadership generation is honestly committed to a "peaceful development", the possibility that future Chinese leaders - from a more powerful position - will introduce a new Chinese development policy, a potentially more ambitious and aggressive one, cannot be ruled out (Kissinger 2011, 512).

The debate about future scenarios for US-China relations reveals the crux of the matter: uncertainty about each other's intentions and deep-rooted distrust on both sides exerts negative influence on the relationship and legitimises deterrence and military hedging. As a result, the US and China become ever more assertive, which in turn raises distrust. The prospect that the US and China could unintentionally get caught in a security dilemma is very real. Politicians on both sides of the pacific already realised that addressing strategic distrust is key to a better understanding, but so far failed to establish trust regarding long-term intentions (Lieberthal and Jisi 2012).

However, strategic distrust has not yet led to a confrontation. Neither China's territorial ambitions in the South and East China Sea nor America's increased military presence in East Asia as part of the so called "pivot to Asia" triggered serious counteractions. This is not to say the freedom of navigation operations by the US Navy in the South China Sea that lead to regular standoffs with the PLA Navy are harmless. However, given the explosive nature of China's territorial claims and the US pivot, these standoffs are a rather modest outcome. Despite mutual distrust US-China relations continue to feature a high level of prudence and restraint. This raises the question what the factors are that exert restraint on the parties and prevent a more confrontational relationship?

A possible explanation is provided by the influence of economic relations. In contrast to political relations, which gradually cooled-off over the last decade, economic relations between the two biggest economies in the world remain strong. Even despite the introduction of higher tariffs by the US and China in 2018 the bilateral trade volume continued to grow. Bilateral economic exchange is and will continue to be vital for both economies. The US is by far China's most important trading partner. In 2016 exports to the US were stagnating but caught up again in the meantime. In 2018 China exported

8,6% more to the US than in the previous year (National Bureau of Statistics of China 2019). For the US, trade vis-a-vis China also has a higher volume than vis-a-vis any other country. However, it is worth pointing out that this is mainly due to the very high number of imports from China to the US. When it comes to US exports China ranks on third place behind the United States' neighbours Canada and Mexico (U.S. Department of Commerce 2017).

Table 1: USA-China Trade Volume in Goods since 1998

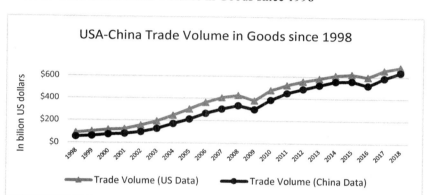

Source: (UN Comtrade 2018)

The economic nexus between China and the US is not limited to trade, but also features a high level of reciprocal investments and holdings of treasury securities. As China exports more to the United States than the USA export to China, it generates considerable savings from the trade surplus. A large part of these savings have been used by Beijing to buy US government securities. By doing so China basically lends the United States money for continued government spending and subsequently also to buy more Chinese products. This enables the United States to spend and consume more than they could normally afford and still maintain low interest rates at the same time (Ferguson and Schularick 2007, 227–30).

As long as the United States want to make new debts anyways, this economic cycle is beneficial for both sides. China can grow its economy through exports and the United States can refinance its national budget at favourable conditions and Americans can enjoy a higher standard of living. This symbiotic economic relationship developed during the first decade of the 21st century and was first described by Ferguson and Schularick in 2007 under the term "Chimerica". The analogy to the mythical hybrid creature Chimera, which combined parts of a lion, a goat and a snake, might or might not be intended by the authors (Ferguson and Schularick 2007, 1–2).

Many academics and economists predicted that "Chimerica" would be a short-lived marriage. They argued that high trade imbalances and rising US debts would not be sustainable. Ferguson and Schularick themselves published an article titled "The End of Chimerica" in 2009 (Ferguson and Schularick 2011). The financial crisis of 2007-2009 seemed to proof them right. Bilateral trade volumes fell in 2009 but this marked only a short downturn in the relationship and not the end of "Chimerica". Trade ties recovered quickly, and the symbiotic relationship continued. In 2018 the US trade deficit with China reached a new high of 419 billion US dollars (United States Census Bureau 2019). China has been the largest foreign holder of US government debt since 2009. And while China reduced its stock of US government securities in 2016, it increased its portfolio again during 2017. By the end of 2018 China held more than 1,1 trillion US dollars in government securities which equals roughly 5,5 of all US debt (U.S. Department of the Treasury 2018b).

This long-lasting economic marriage not only fostered private business ties but also generated an extensive web of economic interdependences. In fact, economic interdependence between the US and China is so high that a discontinuation of economic relations would seriously harm both countries. Already a minor restriction to trade exchange would result in painful opportunity costs. And not only America and China would suffer but the whole world economy would feel the consequences since "Chimerica" now accounts for more than 34% of world GDP and 20% of international trade (Ferguson and Xu 2018, 239–40).

Both sides have an interest to avoid opportunity costs and preserve the gains they receive from commercial interaction. Since a deterioration of political relations can have negative effects on economic relations, there is an incentive to abstain from political confrontation. This logic is the basis for theories on the relationship between interdependence and conflict. Advocates of commercial liberalism assume a positive causality and claim that economic interdependence has a mitigating effect on conflictual political relations.

The next chapter will examine theories of commercial liberalism which describe how economic interdependencies can have a peace-promoting effect on political relations. It will also explore theories that criticise commercial liberalism and asses how these theoretical constructs can be applied to current international relations. Chapter 2.2 will discuss how economic interdependencies have increased and evolved over time and why participating in global free trade has become essential for the development and prosperity of countries in modern times. Based on commercial liberalism theory Chapter 3 will outlay a relationship model which will help to operationalise the analysis of economic interdependencies and incentives for cooperation between China and the United States. Chapter 4 consists of the empirical analysis of all dimensions of economic interdependencies across business sectors. The findings are subsequently discussed in chapter 5. Chapter 5 will also contrast the findings with current political realities, explain how economic interdependencies influence political decision making and which limitations there are. Chapter 6 will pay tribute to human factors in political decision making and further explain the limitations of economic interdependence theory.

2 Theory

2.1 The Theoretical Foundation of Economic Interdependence

Liberalism has a long tradition in developing arguments in favour of a pacifying effect of trade. Montesquieu is considered to be the first to hold the view that international trade promotes peace. In his book *The Spirit of the Laws* (1748) Montesquieu argues that

"the natural effect of commerce is to lead to peace. Two nations that trade together become mutually dependent: if one has an interest in buying, the other has an interest in selling; and all unions are based on mutual needs." (cited in Hirschman 1977, 80)

By claiming that nations who trade with each other become mutually dependent, Montesquieu developed the first theory of economic interdependence. For him interdependence results from the gains that both sides receive from commercial interactions. If trade flows are interrupted both sides would be deprived of the benefits from their trade relations. Trade revenues would be lost and goods that one nation is unable to produce or extract from their natural resources could no longer be acquired from its trading partner. So once commercial relationships are established, both sides have an interest in preserving economic exchange in order to protect their gains. This in turn makes them more likely to avoid conflict as this would interrupt trade and lower their gains (Mansfield and Pollins 2001, 836).

While Montesquieu assumed that trade has a generally positive effect on conflict prevention, he did not claim that trade alone would be enough to end military disputes and rid the world of war. On the contrary, he also mentioned that under certain conditions, commercial relations could lead to jealousy and rivalry, thus bringing nations into conflict with each other (Howse 2006, 1–2).

The German Philosopher Immanuel Kant was more optimistic about the possibility to achieve a status of *perpetual peace* through economic exchange; though only within an alliance of republican states bound together by international law and international organisations (Kant 1795). Kant claims there is a "spirit of commerce" within every human being since it is in human nature to strive for prosperity. As trade promotes prosperity, people will automatically engage in business with each other once granted the freedom of movement and trade (Brandt 2011, 103–4). This "spirit of commerce", however, is "incompatible with war" because war disturbs trade and destroys prosperity. Therefore "the power of money" would constrain people and states likewise to go to war (Kant 1795, 33).

In contrast to Montesquieu, Kant's theory of capitalist peace is not based on bilateral interdependence but argues on the systemic level. It is not the mutual dependence of single states which tempers their belligerence. Actors are rather dependent on the stability of the whole international economic system that allows the "spirit of commerce" to unfold freely and brings prosperity to everybody. For their own self-interest every nation should promote peace as a means to preserve the world trade system (Kant 1795, 33). Since conflict between any two nations harms the entire system and reduces the gains for every nation, international mutual interdependence between all nations emerges once extensive global trade ties are established. Thus, maximum gains, which Kant claims people strive for by nature, can only be achieved when nations act with reserve and avoid conflict. For Kant, the peacemaking effect of trade is based on the people's desire for prosperity and the their "spirit of commerce" (Kant 1795, 33).

The idea that free trade rather than war, conquest and control of foreign trade leads to prosperity was supported by Adam Smith. Smith strongly criticised mercantilism and aggressive foreign trade policies, which were practised by European empires in the 18th century. He held the view that it was more beneficial for the commercial interests of a nation to interact in free trade with its neighbours than attempting to impoverish them by exhausting trade wars. If commercial policies do not focus on getting an edge over competitors, but instead focus on promoting free and undisrupted economic exchange, every nation could develop its full potential and overall gains would increase (Blainey 2013, 302–3).

Smith's compatriot Richard Cobden and other members of the Manchester School of commercial liberalism shared Smith's economic and political beliefs and continued to advocate the advantages of free trade. Cobden expected free trade to empower merchants and businessmen, who he believed to be more peace loving then the political elites. After all, merchants and businessmen are the ones who have the most to lose from a conflict. An empowerment of merchants would not only increase the voice of reason in government but also reduce the political influence of the aristocracy, thus making it harder for political elites to gather public support for conflicts, raise armies and conduct wars (McMillan 1997, 37).

Cobden also consented with Kant and his believe that trade brings nations into a relationship of economic interdependence. Since trade relations between European nations increased drastically in the 19th century, he claimed that a state of economic interdependence had already been achieved (Cain 1979, 234). The increased costs of war in an interdependent world would make war anachronistic, Cobden argued, wherefore he called trade "the grand panacea":

"once people realised that their wealth and prosperity depends on other nations, they would not be willing to harm themselves by fighting their trade partners and bear the costs of it." (Cobden 1903, 36)

As can be seen from the above, theories on the peacemaking effect of trade and economic interdependence are numerous. There are further scholars who refined and extended these theories, but the most important arguments have been presented in this section. Getting an understanding of the lines of argumentation, the reasoning behind those theories and the causal mechanisms is necessary in order to examine their applicability to US-China relations. After the empirical analysis of trade relations and economical interdependencies between China and the United States it will be assessed if theories of commercial liberalism have significance for the current state of bilateral relations and if they can help to explain the various considerations decision makers on both sides of the pacific have to factor in.

While there is a vast amount of liberal theories about the positive effects of free trade and economic interdependence, it must also be taken into account that there is an equally old tradition of arguments against the peacemaking effect of liberal economics. Above all, Marxist proponents, most prominently among them Vladimir Lenin, have always doubted the logic of capitalist peace. In his basic work *Imperialism: The highest stage of capitalism* Lenin expressed that:

"certain bourgeois writers [...] give the hope of peace among nations under capitalism. Theoretically, this opinion is absurd, while in practice it is sophistry and dishonest defense of the worst opportunism." (Lenin 1970, 74)

Typical arguments are that trade and economic development do not decrease the possibility of warfare, but increase conflict by setting nations into competition and causing demands for more economic growth. Nations may be inclined to achieve more growth through forceful annexation of territory and could get into conflict with other nations over territorial claims and rare resources. Furthermore, states might be encouraged to protect trade monopolies by force (Gartzke and Lupu 2012, 120).

Another argument is that economic interdependence will not create a balanced relationship between nations because states are not satisfied with mutual gains, but always seek the highest possible benefit from commercial relations. The strive for maximum gains awakes a nation's desire to come out on top and dominate its trading partners. Following this line of argumentation, economic ties can have a negative effect on political relations and lead to increased competition and rivalry (Gartzke and Lupu 2012, 120).

The main difference between theories predicting a positive effect and those predicting a negative effect of economic interdependence is the thinking in absolute versus relative gains. Proponents of commercial liberalism argue that nations are encouraged to cooperate and enter into economic interdependencies with each other because trade and economic exchange generate a maximum of absolute gains for all nations. On its own a nation can only increase its prosperity to a certain degree but if two or more nations decide to cooperate each of them can achieve higher economic growth. The gains from cooperation can be unevenly distributed, i.e. one country can achieve higher growth than its trading partner, but every nation will be wealthier than without cooperation. Over time, countries who cooperate will become interdependent and as everybody profits from this constellation nations are incentivised not to jeopardise their gains by entering into conflict with economic partners.

Critics of commercial liberalism do not so much question that economic exchange generates mutual gains but argue that nations think in relative gains. They assume that nations will always try to profit more from cooperation than other nations. Nations will engage in trade to achieve higher prosperity but will not be satisfied until their gains are higher than everybody else's gains. A nation that profits less from cooperation than its trading partners will try to alter the conditions of economic exchange and even be willing to jeopardise gains and accept losses in prosperity as long as the losses for everybody else are higher. According to critics of commercial liberalism, even resorting to force can be logical as this could increase the relative gains of an actor.

The thinking in absolute versus relative gains results from different paradigms of a nation and its purpose. Is the goal of a nation, i.e. the driving force for state actions, to achieve higher prosperity and socio-economic development or to dominate other nations and to come out on top? It seems that these paradigms are mutually exclusive and depending on once world view one will assume the best or the worst. However, nations are not abstract constructs but consist of people and people are the ones who decide what purpose their nation should have. Thus, it is entirely possible that some nations think in relative gains while others think in absolute gains. Since the mindset of people in one nation will probably not be totally consistent and can also change over time, the thinking of a nation is also not consistent and may change depending on various circumstances. Consequently, it seems more likely that nations not exclusively think in absolute or relative gains but rather are motivated by both, achieving higher prosperity while also trying to come out on top if possible. Some may be more motivated by the first while others are more motivated by the later. This would also explain why not all nations value economic cooperation equally high.

So maybe after all the paradigms are not mutually exclusive but can be combined. It is beyond question that global economic exchange does not only generate benefits but also creates competition between nations. However, competitors can still decide to cooperate if that is advantageous for everybody. Commercial liberalists argue that they will do so as long as the gains are not too unevenly distributed. If certain nations profit much less from cooperation than other nations it seems reasonable to assume that this could create jealousies and the disadvantaged nation could be inclined to cancel cooperation. This is one of the constellations Montesquieu identified as dangerous, raising the fear that jealousies could bring nations into rivalry; see page 16.

But a constellation of very uneven economic cooperation would mean that economic interdependencies are asymmetrical. When commercial liberals talk about economic interdependence, they mean a constellation in which actors depend on each other roughly equally. If economic interdependencies are too asymmetric, they will not have the effect described by commercial liberalism. In order to have a positive effect, economic cooperation has to be fair for all involved actors and make trading partners similarly dependent. Consequently, the first step to test if economic interdependence theory can be applied to Sino-American relations is to assess if economic dependencies between China and the United States are more or less in balance. Chapter four will discuss all dimensions of economic dependencies in detail, thus allowing to determine how symmetric economic relations between China and the United States are.

2.2 Economic Interdependence in Modern Times

While at the time of the First World War territorial annexation as a means to enlarge an empire and increase a nation's power was still a possible foreign policy option, though not necessarily the most beneficial, this approach towards development has become unthinkable in today's time. Almost all former colonies have been returned and the success of separatist movements all over the world have led to the formation of innumerable new countries, of which most are rather small in size. Thus, the average size of countries is declining. The age of empires big enough to be self-sufficient and independent of interstate commercial activities has passed. In modern times countries are obliged to engage in trade in order to achieve economic growth and to obtain all goods it cannot provide from its own resources or domestic production. The prosperity of countries rests on interactions with other countries as much as never before. Interdependence has become inevitable (Rosecrance 2013, 354–55). Countries which tried alternative strategies of development and deployed economic policies of sell-sufficiency and self-dependence have failed, as the examples of North Korea and China before the economic opening demonstrate. China has been afflicted by famines during times of isolation, most notably the Great Chinese Famine from 1959 to 1961, and North Korea still experiences food shortages and starvation (Cumings 2005, 436–46).

To achieve a fair level of wealth and to supply its citizens and companies with all required goods and resources, states find themselves compelled to open their borders for international commercial interactions. Progress in transportation and industry have made trade and production even more profitable in comparison to territorial conquest and exploitation. Thus, an aggressive military foreign policy aimed at exploiting other countries has become much less appealing than to engage in peaceful economic cooperation (Rosecrance 2013, 356).

The development towards a world-wide free trade regime was accompanied by a drastic increase of international economic exchange and investment flows. During the two decades after the Second World War international trade multiplied and rose from approximately 45 billion US dollars in 1945 to about 165 billion US dollars in 1965. One of the first to realise that this increase in commercial intercourse was not simply resulting in more interconnectedness, but was also causing significant reciprocal sensitivities among countries, was Richard Cooper in 1968 (Cooper 1968: 59-60). Cooper observed that the more commercial interaction grew, the more economic development and policy decisions in one country affected the national economies of other countries. Due to increased interconnectedness, an economic crisis in one part of the world can more easily spread to other regions. What Cooper described was not only interdependence in the sense of dependence on undisturbed trade, but in the sense of external forces profoundly influencing all economic affairs of otherwise sovereign countries (Cooper 1968, 76–77).

He presents three reasons for the rapid expansion of trade activities: changes in commercial policies, a reduction of transportation costs and "broader business horizons". First, a new emphasis on free trade after the Second World War led to the reduction of tariff barriers and other artificial trade barriers, which enabled easier and more profitable commercial exchange. Second, due to innovations in ocean shipping, a general rise in prices, and transportation of more valuable cargo instead of primary goods, transportation costs dropped drastically relative to the value of the shipped goods. This development had an even stronger effect on the increase of world trade than changes in commercial policies since transportation costs often exceeded custom duties on many kinds of products. As third cause for the rapid growth of international trade Cooper identified a new openness of businessmen for the development of new markets. As the world was becoming more interconnected, new opportunities opened up and business horizons broadened. As a result, an increasing amount of companies ran the risk to expand to new markets, eventually leading to an increase in world trade volume as well as in foreign direct investments (Cooper 1968, 63–68).

Consequently, trade flows increased, but at the same time they became notably more sensitive towards fluctuations regarding e.g. costs, incomes, prices, or exchange rates. Thus, a reduction in production costs in country A would have an immediate effect on the trade balance with other countries and deteriorate their position in the market relative to country A. In other words, changes in one country affect other countries much faster and more fiercely when barriers of distance and tariffs are low. When sensitivity is high, meaning that changes in one country lead to effects in other countries, all countries become interdependent. Therefore Cooper concluded that in the wake of changes in transportation, commercial policies and business horizons, the responsiveness towards external factors increased, which led to a state of higher sensitivity and thus created economic interdependence (Cooper 1968, 76–77 & 148).

Cooper himself qualified his analysis in one important point. Trading activities increased particularly between industrial countries. Trading networks grew unequally, leaving some regions barely connected to the rest of the world. Those countries poorly integrated in the world-wide free trade order were also less sensitive to changes from abroad. Hence, economic interdependence was limited to the industrialised world in 1968 (Cooper 1968, 59 & 148).

Cooper's findings of a world economy in transition and his observation of increased economic interdependence were shared by many academics. Subsequently, interdependence theory experienced a renaissance in the 1970s. Several scholars, the majority belonging to the liberal school, extended interdependence theory and conducted research on the dynamics and effects of economic interdependence: most famously Robert Keohane and Joseph Nye in their 1977 book *Power and Interdependence: World Politics in Transition*. As the title suggests, Keohane and Nye examined the influence of interdependence on power. While in the traditional realist thinking power derives from military force and is the exclusive domain of state actors, interdependence increases the importance of economic power and grants significant power to non-state actors too. When state power is insufficient to ensure economic development, states are compelled to engage in trade and build linkages with other countries. In doing so, states relinquish control and power to civil actors, who are involved in the commercial activities with other countries (Keohane and Nye 1989, 3–5).

However, Keohane and Nye were not suggesting that states would completely lose their position as dominant actors in the international system and be replaced by transnational corporations, social movements, and international organisations but rather claimed that power was shifting only gradually. They were also sceptical about the idea that interdependence necessarily leads to cooperation and would make power politics become outdated. While they acknowledged that military power had become inappropriate or impracticable in many circumstances (e.g. military conflict within the Western World has become unthinkable and the United States were unable to win the Vietnam War despite their military dominance), they also considered that other forms of power, e.g. economic power, could just as likely evoke conflicts. In their view interdependence would merely end traditional forms of conflict, making military disputes between interdependent states obsolete, but simultaneously foster new forms and features of conflict (Keohane and Nye 1989, 3–8 & 27–29).

Especially asymmetric interdependencies bear the danger of conflictual relationships. If external factors affect some actors, state or non-state, notably less than others, they are less dependent. Their resilience against change is higher from which results power because they would bear less costs from altered circumstances and thus could achieve a comparative advantage from initiating change themselves (Keohane and Nye 1989, 11). Since opportunity costs are uneven in a relationship of asymmetric interdependence, it can be concluded that the respective restraint will also be uneven. Consequently, if economic interdependence is too asymmetric, it may lose its pacifying effect or even encourage less dependent states to take advantage of their resilience. This suggests, as has already been discussed in the previous chapter, that large asymmetries in economic interdependence can have negative effects on interstate relations and may even make conflict more likely. However, which degree of asymmetry would reverse the logic of economic interdependence is unclear and not proven until now.

Another contribution from Keohane and Nye to the study of interdependence is the differentiation of economic interdependence in different dimensions. As already pointed out, states are increasingly dependent on foreign commerce. More precisely interdependence can express itself in sensitivities to external factors. Sensitivity interdependence describes the responsiveness of a country towards changes from abroad. But even costly changes do not necessarily need to have extensive negative consequences if a state can compensate these changes or adapt quickly to the new situation. A state that has oil reserves and the know-how to exploit them will not suffer the same consequences from an oil shortage as states without these capabilities. At first every state will be affected by an oil shortage - some more and some less, depending on their import volume, which again is the indicator for their sensitivity - but a state with own oil reserves has the ability to adjust to the altered circumstances and replace the oil imports with own supplies. After an adaptation time, the negative consequences for these states will decrease. However, if a state has no capabilities to absorb the consequences of changed economic conditions, it faces the entire financial burden, and thus is not only sensitive, but also vulnerable to external factors (Keohane and Nye 1989, 12–14).

This distinction between sensitivity and vulnerability interdependence is important, because mere sensitivity interdependence is not as relevant for the study of interdependence and conflict as vulnerability interdependence. If opportunity costs are only temporary, they will have a less restraining effect as long lasting costs. A state which is only interdependent in the dimension of sensitivity can, in a sense, dissolve its interdependencies by making adjustments to its domestic economy. Though in most cases the adjusted situation will not be as beneficial as the status quo because otherwise a country would not have engaged in economic exchange in the first place. Some negative effects like e.g. higher domestic production costs will even remain but consequences will not be as severe as for states with a high level of vulnerability interdependence. Vulnerability interdependence cannot be dissolved as easily. States can only try to become less vulnerable in the long run but that is always accompanied by opportunity costs because substituting or diversifying supply chains require investments. If domestic substitution is not possible and if also no or not enough alternative suppliers are available, dissolving economic interdependencies even becomes impossible (Keohane and Nye 1989, 15).

With this differentiation in mind, it becomes clear that some indicators for economic interdependence are not as convincing as others. For example, high import rates alone merely indicate a high sensitivity interdependence. A state only becomes vulnerable when it is incapable to compensate an absence of imports. In the examination of economic interdependencies this distinction between sensitivities and vulnerabilities must be considered. It will be necessary to differentiate which dimensions of interdependence exist between China and the United States and how pronounced they are for certain economic sector in order to determine how strong economic interdependencies impact Sino-American relations.

The findings of Cooper, Keohane, Nye and other scholars improved the understanding of economic interdependence and revealed a much more complex mode of operation and more sophisticated mechanisms of economic interdependence than the basic theories suggested. They observed a world that had become deeply influenced by economic interdependence but realised that interdependence is unevenly distributed among countries and has many different dimensions. Considering the complexity of the subject, high accuracy is needed when the interaction of economic interdependence and conflict is being examined. Therefore, this study will not solely rely on mathematic models (e.g. trade volume as percentage of GDP) like many other studies do because they are not able to display and capture the complexity of the effects of economic interdependence. Instead, this study will only use statistical models in the first part of the analysis and then focus on examining the different dimensions and effects of economic interdependence separately and across all economic interactions between China and the United States.

Despite the prevailing assumption that the world entered an era of interdependence after the Second World War, some scholars denied the expansion of economic interdependencies and the increasing importance of economic power. Especially scholars associated with realism like Kenneth Waltz claimed that increased interconnectedness was not leading to an increased and meaningful economic interdependence. Waltz admitted that economics shocks spread faster due to advantages in communication and transportation but would have only minor effects on states because vulnerabilities had declined. In fact, he claimed that the most powerful states after the Second World War were significantly less interdependent than the dominant states in the era before World War One. As evidence he compared the value of imports and exports relative to the overall GDP, known as the trade openness ratio, of the most important European states at the beginning of the 20th century with the trade openness of the USA and the USSR in 1975; see table 1. He argues the high difference in the meal value, 47,5% for European powers at the beginning of the 20th century and 11% for the USA and the USSR in 1975, demonstrates the shrinking importance of interdependence (Waltz 2013, 339–45).

Table 2: Exports plus Imports as a Percentage of GDP

1909-13	U.K., France, Germany, Italy	33-52%
1975	USA, Soviet Union	8-14%

Source: (Waltz 2013, 340)

Proponents of interdependence like Cooper object that figures like these are misleading and that economic interdependence before World War One was somewhat an "illusion" because long distances and slow transportation acted as "natural barriers" and made trade undynamic to the point that external changes only affected other countries in the long run; giving them time to adjust (Cooper 1968, 150–53). Additionally, as already mentioned above, imports and exports alone are not very convincing indicators for economic interdependence. If a state can compensate a reduction in imports or exports, it will not suffer high costs. In order to obtain a more precise assessment of interdependencies one would have to examine the product categories being traded and assess how important they are for the national economy. Luxury goods, for example, are not as important for a country as for instance raw materials. In fact, luxury goods made up a large portion of trade between Germany and the United Kingdom before World War One (Blanchard and Ripsman 1996). It would have been necessary to analyse how vulnerable and not only how sensitive the respective states have been to a discontinuation of trade ties to attain a more realistic assessment of interdependencies between European powers before World War One.

However, trade value as share of GDP, the trade openness ratio, is a good first indicator for economic interdependence. Some meaningful degree of foreign trade is necessary in order to suffer opportunity costs high enough to give enough incentive for preserving peaceful relations with trading partners (Oneal and Russet 1997, 271–72).

As pointed out by Waltz, economic interdependencies appear only moderately strong in the year 1975. However, it is not very representative to examine only the two opposing superpowers at that time. Figures from only 4 years later, which include further major industrial countries, give a different picture as can be seen from table 2.

Table 3: Sum of Exports and Imports as a Percentage of GDP for the Largest National Economies in 1979

1979	USA, Japan, Germany, U.K., France	9-26%

Source: (Stewart 1984, 21)

Trade openness in industrial countries in 1979 had already reached a level which would have made the interruption of trade flows considerably costly. As was predicted by liberal scholars, the trend continued and more recent figures from 2016 suggest a very integrated world economy.

Table 4: Sum of Exports and Imports as a Percentage of GDP for the Largest National Economies in 2016

Ranking GDP (PPP)	Country	Ex.+ Im./ GDP
1	USA	19,9%
2	China	17,2%
3	India	7,1%
4	Japan	23,8%
5	Germany	59,4%
6	Russia	13,8%
Average Value	Top 6 economies	23,5%

Source: (UN Comtrade 2018) (The World Bank 2017)

As can be seen from table 3, foreign trade has become very important for the economic performance of the largest national economies in the world, i.e. the United States, China, India, Japan, Germany, and Russia. This indicates that economic interdependencies have increased drastically and are as strong as never before. It is also striking that the dependence on trade varies distinctly even among industrial states and not only between industrial and developing countries as Cooper observed in the 1960s. India has a trade openness ratio of only 7,1% which means it is not yet fully integrated into world trade flows whereas Germany has a very high trade openness ratio of 59,4% which means that the German economy is very dependent on foreign trade exchange. The United States and China have a more average trade openness ratio of 19,9% and 17,2% respectively which shows that they are both almost equally deeply connect to the world economy. Compared to the trade openness ratio of the two largest economies in 1975, the United States and the Soviet Union, which had a trade openness of 14% and 8%, the United States and China have a 7,5% higher exposure to global trade in 2016.

The rapid increase in world-wide trade activities and the acceleration of economic integration that the world experienced in the last years is referred to as *globalisation* (di Mauro, Dees, and McKibbin 2008, 5). While there is no consistency in the definition of globalisation, it is mainly used synonymously with interdependence. Since the 1990s it has widely replaced the term interdependence to describe the ongoing trend of increasing economic openness and interconnectedness. Globalisation differs from interdependence only in its extensity, intensity, velocity, and impact. Colloquially, globalisation can be called "the big brother of economic interdependence", although it has still the same meaning: events in one part of the world have ramifications for others. Globalisation even reinforced reciprocal effects among states by creating "thick networks of interdependence" (Keohane 2002, 14). The formation of these "thick networks" was a simultaneous development which led to deeper regionalisation in addition to more global interconnectedness. Economic integration increased on a global scale, but it increased even faster within geographic regions. Both, globalisation and regionalisation "made domestic economies more sensitive to global and regional developments" (di Mauro, Dees, and McKibbin 2008, 14). Thus, in addition to increased global interdependencies, specific regional interdependencies evolved.

In contrast to earlier stages of economic integration, one feature has by far become more important. Economic globalisation in modern times is not just characterised by an extensive exchange of goods, but also introduced outsourcing as common business practice. Production centres have been translocated all over the world with the objective to reduce production costs. Additionally, a vast amount of goods is not produced at a single place anymore. More often components of a final product are built in different parts of the world and are assembled in yet another part (di Mauro, Dees, and McKibbin 2008, 9).

This manufacturing process, which is based on global supply chains, achieves a high productivity, but is also very sensitive to disturbances. If one link of the chain breaks down, it has negative effects for the entire production circle including all companies and states involved. Thus, global supply chains are fostering economic interdependencies. On the basis of this logic, Thomas Friedman has develop the "Dell Theory of Conflict Prevention" which constitutes that "no two countries that are both part of a major global supply chain, like Dell's [supply chain of electronic components], will ever fight a war against each other as long as they are both part of the same global supply chain" (Friedman 2005, 421). Friedman argues that global supply chains are of fundamental importance for the development of poorer countries and the prosperity of more developed countries. Countries and their people alike would not be willing to jeopardise their wellbeing by conducting wars, which would disconnect them from the world economy and drive off investments (Friedman 2005, 421–22).

In addition to the outsourcing of production and services, another form of international division of labour has been established. Following the logic of Ricardo's theory on comparative advantages that specialisation will lead to overall gains, countries increasingly specialise on the production of certain goods which they can produce more efficiently than other countries. Speciali-sation reinforces interdependencies of global supply chains since the imports from one country cannot as simply be compensated with equivalent imports from another country anymore. Certain components are even exclusively produced in a single country and nowhere else. As a consequence the global economy has become very vulnerable and the disconnection of even just a single country from the global economy can have major ramifications for supply chains across almost all economic sectors (Friedman 2005, 225–36).

The aspect that the international division of labour increases interdepend-encies is very relevant for this study since the United States and China are part of some of the most important global supply chains. It will be examined if their involvement in supply chains increases the vulnerability of the United States and China, thus giving more incentive for continued cooperation.

Economic interdependencies have increased drastically over the last decades due to different developments and phenomena, resulting in strong sensitivity interdependencies as well as vulnerability interdependencies. Economic in-teraction with foreign countries has become a necessity to achieve faster economic development. Every country is, to a certain degree, connected to foreign markets and thus affected by external forces. Those countries, which are deeply involved in global economic processes are the most dependent ones. The economic performance of these countries relies heavily on foreign trade and investments. Any circumstance which would compromise world trade flows would have serious consequences for their national economies. Therefore, industrial countries like the United States and China seems to have a high incentive to avoid conflicts and to preserve the global free-trade re-gime.

3 Model Construction and Research Design

As has been laid on in the previous chapter, the causal mechanics of economic interdependence are complex and there are several dimensions in which they can influence state behaviour. To facilitate the analysis of economic interdependencies between China and the United States this study will first introduce a model of US-China relations. In order to visualise relations in a comprehensible way that allows drawing conclusions on influencing factors, a relationship model is needed which is limited to the most basic characteristics. A common method to analytically display a phenomenon is constructing an ideal type scenario. An ideal type is an exaggeration of reality with the objective to facilitate the description and examination of a social phenomenon (Weber 1949, 90). In the following an ideal type relationship model for Sino-American relations is developed to get a better understanding of US-China relations and how economic interdependence can impact political relations.

In the most simplified scenario of a relationship actors only have two options. They can either choose to cooperate or to head for confrontation. Every option in between is a mixture of cooperative strategies and confrontational ones. Neutrality is achieved when cooperation and confrontation are in perfect balance. In fact, the very meaning of the word neutrality, deriving from the Latin word *"neutrum"*, is being "neither" of anything. Thus, neutrality can only exist in between two poles. In real relationships, however, actual neutrality is impossible to achieve. Even Switzerland, which is considered the prime example of a neutral country, cooperates more with some countries than with others. Thus, we assume that relationship always tend towards one pole on the cooperation-confrontation scale.

Since all possible relationship scenarios can be displayed as a combination of more or less conflict and cooperation – e.g. 50% cooperation and 50% confrontation for neutrality – a model of bilateral relations can be constructed with only these two characteristics. The result is two by two matrix that has the layout of a game theory matrix; see table 4.

The two basic options, cooperation and confrontation, are located on the outside of the matrix and the outcomes for each combination of options are located in the inside. As there are four possible combinations – (1) US Cooperation & China Cooperation , (2) US Cooperation & China Confrontation, (3) US Confrontation & China Cooperation, (4) US Confrontation & China Confrontation), there are also four basic outcomes, which give information about the nature of US-China relations in each scenario. Obviously, more than four outcomes are conceivable, but these four constitute the most basic and pure ideal types of possible relationships. One could easily add a scale ranging from 100% cooperation to 100% confrontation to each axis of the model, thus displaying all possible options and outcomes. However, for the purpose of analysability the model is kept as simple as possible.

Table 5: US-China Relationship Model

		China	
		Engagement (Cooperation)	Confrontation
USA	Engagement (Cooperation)	Power Sharing (Peaceful Rise)	Appeasement (Chinese Superiority, Tianxia)
	Confrontation	Containment (Preservation of Hegemony)	Escalating Strategic Competition and High Risk of Conflict (Power Transition Fight)

(Source: self-provided graphic)

The ideal type relationship model in Table 6 can be used to analyse past and current policies as well as to make assumptions about future relationship scenarios. US-China relations before 1969 have been quasi non-existed. They would best be described as neutral since there was neither much cooperation nor much confrontation. With the US-China rapprochement in the 1970s cooperation between the US and China increased and the nature of US-China relations increasingly approximated relationship scenario one in the upper left of the model. This process was accompanied by economic gains for both sides and a gradual liberalisation of Chinese politics and society. Proponents of commercial liberalism, as was described in the previous chapters, favour continued cooperation as a way to preserve gains and to promote China's integration into the current world order.

Where US-China relations are heading is the centre of debate among politicians, China experts and scholars of international relations. What seems to be common sense, however, is that relations are not anymore characterised by high cooperation alone but started to move from the upper left scenario of mutual cooperation towards one of the other three scenarios; see table 6.

People who see China as a potential revisionist power and criticise America's engagement policies as appeasement are afraid that China will supersede the US as the world's sole super power in the near future and strive for the restoration of the old Chinese world order of "Tianxia", meaning "all under heaven", with China constituting the heavenly kingdom on top of all other nations. This would be scenario two in the upper right.

People who believe in China's peaceful development and interpret America's pivot to Asia as a containment strategy think that the US wants to preserve its hegemony at all cost and assume that the US will ultimately confront China in order to keep it down. This would be scenario three in the lower left.

Advocates of power transition theory assume that the US will try to contain China, while China will try to acquire economic as well as military superiority. As was discussed above, in this scenario the uncertainty about each other's intentions is said to result in an escalating strategic competition, which bears a high risk of conflict and can possibly even lead to war. This would be scenario four in the lower right.

Scenario one is favourable for both countries as this would preserve mutual gains. Scenario two is favourable for China as this would allow China to achieve political hegemony. Scenario three is favourable for the United States as this would preserve the current world order and US hegemony. Scenario four is unfavourable for both because confrontation endangers mutual gains but would ensure that neither of the two countries could win the upper hand anytime soon.

Table 6: US-China Relationship Model

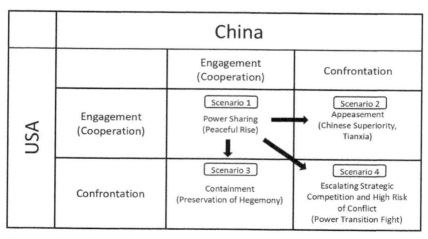

(Source: self-provided graphic)

The US-China relationship model has much in common with a paradox in game theory known as the prisoner's dilemma. In a situation in which two prisoners would be best of if both would give no evidence, it is still very likely that they will incriminate each other for fear of defection by their partner (Jervis 1978, 171). For the US and China, too, cooperation would be the best choice, but if only one of them chooses to continue cooperation while the other one opts for confrontational policies, the one who chose cooperation will be faced with a unfavourable scenario (i.e. scenario 2 or 3). Since a defection from cooperation cannot be ruled out, both sides might choose to play save, prepare for confrontation and start to take preemptive measures to avoid a disadvantages scenario. The more preemptive measures both players take, e.g. by increasing military capabilities or building alliances, the more suspicious both will get and the more reason both have to be assertive. As this negative spiral effect is unintended and only results from the personal desire for security, it is described as "security dilemma" in Internal Relations (IR) theory.

With regard to US-China relations the question arises whether the US and China are actually at risk of running into a security dilemma? Recent developments in both countries' foreign policy give at least cause for concern. China's quickly growing military budget and the increased capabilities of the People's Liberation Army (PLA) may be understood in China as obligatory investments in national security but worry observers in the Pentagon and the White House. The same is true for America's pivot to Asia. Although not necessarily a containment strategy, but an adaptation to changing global priorities, decision-makers in Beijing are alarmed about increased US military presence in the Asia-Pacific. Every change in the global balance of power is a dangerous high-wire act. Therefore, it is undeniable that the shifting power constellation between the US and China is potentially dangerous. Competition between the US and China grows, thus increasing the probability of disputes and incidents. However, this does not mean that a security dilemma is inevitable as strategies exist to stop the negative spiral dynamic of an escalating competition.

The dynamic of a "security dilemma" between two players is basically the same as in an iterated prisoner's dilemma. As foreign policy is not a one-time decision-making situation, countries can switch between strategies of cooperation and confrontation over time. For an iterated prisoner's dilemma strategies have been developed to escape from the dilemma. Since the "game" now has more than one round, players can learn from their opponent's behaviour and try to encourage cooperation by signalling a benign attitude.

Among various strategies, "tit for tat" is considered the most successful one to avoid a negative spiral effect. This strategy requires from a player to make a cooperative first move in order to show goodwill. If the opponent chooses not to cooperate but to defect, this behaviour must be punished with an equally uncooperative move to signal that confrontation will not pay off. However, once the opponent starts to make concessions this should be credited with a cooperative next move. Practicing forgiveness is important to demonstrate the worthwhileness of cooperation. When a tit for tat pattern is maintained over several rounds one's own behaviour becomes predictable so that an opponent must not fear to be deceived but can expect that cooperative behaviour will be answered with cooperation in reverse. This way trust between players can be established and the security dilemma can be overcome (Jervis 1978, 171).

Essential for the success of this strategy is the goodwill of the actors and their willingness to cooperate with each other. Actors are more likely to cooperate if cooperation pays of and if non-cooperation has negative consequences. This is where economic interdependence comes in. Economic interdependence increases the costs of defection and the payoffs of cooperation. In a situation of economic interdependence, conflict would be accompanied by high costs due to the negative economic ramifications. Another effect is that cooperation becomes symbiotic in a situation of economic interdependence. The synergetic effects of interdependence create a mutual beneficial relationship that is very worthwhile for both sides. Thus, the higher the degree of economic interdependence between two actors, the more rational it is to cooperate.

Table 7: US-China Relationship Scenario Model with Possible Effect of Economic Interdependence

		China	
		Engagement (Cooperation)	Confrontation
USA	Engagement (Cooperation)	Scenario 1 Power Sharing (Peaceful Rise)	Scenario 2 Appeasement (Chinese Superiority, Tianxia)
	Confrontation	Scenario 3 Containment (Preservation of Hegemony)	Scenario 4 Escalating Strategic Competition and High Risk of Conflict (Power Transition Fight)

(Source: self-provided graphic)

Summing up the above, it is hypothesised that while US-China relations are moving from relationship scenario one, mutual cooperation, to other directions - possibly closer to scenario four with the risk of running into a security dilemma - economic interdependence has a diametric effect on US-China relations, which is at least slowing down the negative development and might even be strong enough to keep the relationship in the current scenario; see table 7.

In order to determine the costs of confrontation - and thus the level of incentive for the US and China to continue cooperation - this study will use the concept of complex interdependence by Keohane and Nye since it demonstrates how in a globalised world the fortune of states is inevitably tied together. In their research Keohane and Nye argue that interdependence has two dimensions: sensitivity and vulnerability. While sensitivity interdependence describes a state of mere interconnectedness in which states can look for other countries to compensate for the loss of trading partners, vulnerability interdependence describes a relationship in which both parties are reliant on each other because no other states can provide the goods they need or because other trading partners cannot sufficiently compensate the losses. Confrontation in a state of sensitivity interdependence can already cause considerable costs as compensation often requires adjustments and takes time. But only if states are vulnerable to the actions of other states does conflict or non-cooperation cause very high costs (Keohane and Nye 1989, 12–15).

For US-China relations this means that the more vulnerable the US and China are to disturbances in their economic relations, the higher is the incentive to continue engagement policies and cooperation. In order to test the hypothesis that economic interdependencies incentivise cooperation and have a beneficial effect on Sino-American relations, this study will examine in the following chapter which economic sensitivities and vulnerabilities exist between the US and China. As the level of economic interdependence may vary across numerous fields of bilateral exchange and cooperation, this analysis will be done separately for different economic sectors and areas of cooperation. For all of these areas the level of interdependence will be examined in detail so that an overall picture of all sensitivities and vulnerabilities can be obtained. The results of this analysis will allow making a statement about the level of incentive for cooperation.

4 Economic Interdependencies between the United States and China

4.1 Bilateral Trade Data

The most extensive source for international trade data is the United Nations International Trade Statistics Database (UN Comtrade). It consists of annual international trade reports from 170 countries which are coded and transformed into a UN standard format by the United Nations Statistics Division. For reasons of comparability UN Comtrade converts commodity values from national currency into US dollars using exchange rates supplied by the reporting countries or derived from monthly market rates and volume of trade (UN Trade Statistics 2016).

A well-known problem with trade data is that reported exports from country A to country B very rarely match the reported imports from country B to country A. Logically, the reported export values of a country should mirror the import values of its partner countries since one country's exports are another country's imports but in reality discrepancies can be enormous. The United Nations Statistics Division identified more than 30 reasons for bilateral asymmetries in trade data. Some of the main reasons are listed below:

- Transportation and insurance costs are usually added to the reported import value but are normally excluded from the reported export value
- Partner country attributions differ depending on whether the country of origin is reported or the country of last known location
- Time lag between shipment and arrival can result in the registration of exports in one year while the registration of the corresponding imports only happens in the following year

(UN Trade Statistics 2015)

Trade date from the United States and from China are affected by these problems and do not correspond. While the United States reported imports from China with a total value of 481,5 billion US dollars for the year 2016, China only reported exports with a total value of 385,7 billion US dollar. This discrepancy of 95,8 billion US dollar for "eastbound trade" shows by how much trade data can vary among trading partners. The asymmetry for "westbound trade", i.e. Chinese imports and US exports, is smaller but still amounts to 19,5 billion US dollars. For "westbound trade" and "eastbound trade" alike the import values are higher than the corresponding export values. This means that for the total bilateral trade volume (i.e. volume of imports + exports) the discrepancies offset each other resulting in a variation of 76,3 billion US dollars between US statistics for the total bilateral trade volume (597,1 billion US dollars) and Chinese statistics for the total bilateral trade volume (520,8 billion US dollars) (UN Comtrade 2018).

Table 8: Trade Data Asymmetry between USA and China in 2016

Reporting Country	Eastbound Trade		Westbound Trade		Total Trade Volume
USA	Imports from China	481,5	Exports to China	115,6	597,1
China	Exports to US	385,7	Imports from USA	135,1	520,8
Discrepancy	95,8		-19,5		76,3

In billion US dollars

Source: (UN Comtrade 2018)

Since large trade data asymmetries in Sino-American statistics are a historic problem the US Department of Commerce and the Ministry of Commerce of the People's Republic of China established a joint working group in 2004 to explore causes for the non-conformance of bilateral trade data. In addition to the above-mentioned explanations of the United Nations Statistics Division the Sino-American working group identified the following reasons to be of major significance for the discrepancies between US and Chinese data:

- Shipments via Intermediary Countries: Some goods that are declared as exports to third countries end up in the United States or China. This happens very often with Chinese exports that go first to Hong Kong but are finally shipped to the United States
- Re-exports: Chinese and US export statistics include re-exports of goods that have not originated in China or the US. However, both countries import statistics record re-exports as imports from the country of origin
- Statistical Territory: Puerto Rico and the US Virgin Islands are included in US trade data, while China has separate trade records for these territories

(US & China Statistics Working Group 2012)

The joint working group calculated that 65% of the discrepancy in bilateral trade data for the year 2010 can be attributed to these three reasons alone. In an endeavour to reduce statistical discrepancy the working group adjusted the 2010 data using all identified factors. However, even after adjustments residual discrepancy was still 20%. (US & China Statistics Working Group 2012).

Since even adjusted bilateral trade data is not symmetric, a so-called "mirroring" of the data, i.e. using the United States' data set for US exports to China and US imports from China as data set for Chinese imports from the United States and Chinese exports to the United States, is not possible.

The logical consequence of trade data asymmetries is that no comparison can be drawn between data from different reporters. Comparing reported exports by the United States with reported exports by China or reported imports by China with reported imports by the United States is not meaningful because US and Chinese statistics include different variables. To get meaningful results, the numbers reported by China can only be compared with other Chinese trade data and numbers reported by the United States can only be compared with other US trade data. Therefore, the following analysis uses two separate trade data sets – one from the United States and one from China. For the analysis of US trade with China only American statistics are used and for the analysis of Chinese trade with the United States only Chinese statistics are used. Because of this approach, import, export and total trade volume for the same year will vary throughout the text depending on the reporting country.

4.2 Trade Volume

The trade volume of a country is the sum of all exports and imports with all trading partner countries. Accordingly, bilateral trade volume is the sum of all exports and imports between country a and country b. The volume of trade gives information about how trade-orientated a country is. If the ratio of a country's trade volume to a country's GDP is high, this is seen as evidence for the "openness" of a country for trade since the higher the ratio, the more of the national income is based on foreign trade. For the calculation of the trade openness ratio gross domestic products based on purchasing power parities $(GDP[PPP]_{a,t})$ are used, because exchange rates are known to distort international comparisons involving untradeable goods (Oneal and Russet 1997, 275).

$$\text{Trade Openness Ratio} = \frac{(\text{Exports}_a + \text{Imports}_a)}{GDP[PPP]_a}$$

Calculations based on trade volume data from UN Comtrade (UN Comtrade 2018) and GDP values from the World Bank (The World Bank 2017) result in the following trade openness ratios for the United States and China in the year 2016 (all figures in billion US dollars).

$$USA(a) = \frac{(1450,5 + 2248,2)}{18624,5} = 0,199 \ (19,9\%)$$

$$China(b) = \frac{(2097,6 + 1587,9)}{21450,9} = 0,172 \ (17,2\%)$$

The trade openness ratios for the United States and China reveal that the United States rely more on global trade than China (by 2,7%). However, the figures only get meaningful with the addition of reference values because only a comparison with other countries can tell if 19,9% and 17,2% are high or low ratios and if a difference of 2,7% is significant. The third largest economy in 2016, after China and the United States, was India with a GDP (PPP) of 8717,5 billion US dollars. India's trade openness ratio for 2016 is only 7,1% and thus significantly smaller compared to the United States and China. Thus, India is less dependent on foreign trade than the United States and China and a larger part of its national income is based on the domestic market.

$$India = \frac{(260,3 + 356,7)}{8717,5} = 0,071 \ (7,1\%)$$

Russia, whose national economy is highly dependent on the exports of fossil fuels, has also a smaller trade openness ratio of 13,8%.

$$Russia = \frac{(285,5+182,3)}{3397,4} = 0,138 \ (13,8\%)$$

This comparison shows that the United States' and China's national economies have a relatively high exposure to global trade as a large part of their wealth depends on the economic exchange with other countries. Only very export-oriented countries like Germany (59,4%) or Japan (23,8%) have a higher trade openness ratio. The large range between the trade openness ratios of the largest world economies, from 7,1% for India to 59,4% for Germany, indicates that the ratio difference of 2,7% between the United States and China is not very meaningful. Both countries are similarly dependent on good trade ties with the rest of the world and therefore have a high incentive to preserve stable political relationships in general and in particular with their most important trading partners.

How much of China's and America's economic output depends on bilateral trade with each other cannot be concluded from the trade openness ratios. Therefore, another indicator is needed to describe the economic interdependence between China and the United States. In an extensive literature review on the study of economic interdependencies Mansfield and Pollins describe bilateral trade volume to GDP ratio as "leading indicator" for the importance of trade between two countries (Mansfield and Pollins 2001, 848–49). This view is supported by McMillan's analysis of 20 political and economic studies. A majority uses the bilateral trade to GDP ratio as independent variable to test the correlation between trade and conflict (McMillan 1997). The bilateral trade to GDP ratio is very similar to the trade openness ratio as it divides the sum of a country's exports and imports with its partner by its GDP to create a measure of the economic dependence of the country on these commercial relations (Oneal, Russett, and Berbaum 2003, 377).

UN Comtrade reports the exports of country a to country b (Exports $_{ab,t}$) and the imports of country a from country b (Imports $_{ab,t}$) separately. For the above mentioned reasons the economic importance of bilateral trade is calculated relative to national income in the form of gross domestic products based on purchasing power parity (GDP[PPP]$_{a,t}$). The dependence of country a on trade with country b in year t is described by this formula:

$$\text{Bilateral Trade To GDP Ratio} = \frac{\left(\text{Exports}_{ab,t} + \text{Imports}_{ab,t}\right)}{\text{GDP[PPP]}_{a,t}}$$

Once more trade data sets from UN Comtrade (UN Comtrade 2018) and GDP values from the World Bank (The World Bank 2017) are used to calculate the bilateral trade to GDP ratio (all figures in billion US dollars). The discrepancy in the reported import and export values for the United States and China (Exports $_{ab,t} \neq$ Imports $_{ba,t}$) result from bilateral trade data asymmetries, which have been described in the previous chapter.

$$\text{USA}(a, 2016) = \frac{(115,6 + 481,5)}{18624,5} = 0,0321 \ (3,21\%)$$

$$\text{China}(b, 2016) = \frac{(385,7 + 135,1)}{21450,9} = 0,0243 \ (2,43\%)$$

The trade volume between the United States and China has the size of 3,21% of the United States' GDP (PPP), while it has the size of 2,43% of China's GDP (PPP). These bilateral trade to GDP ratios are the highest both countries have with any trade partner. No other trade relationship is more important for the economic output of both countries, which points to a high level of economic dependency. The next important trade partner for the United States is Canada with a ratio of 2,9% and for China the second in line is Japan with a ratio of 1,3%. While the difference between trade with China and trade with Canada is only 0,31% for the United States, the gap between trade with the United Stated and Japan is 1,13% for China. Thus, the United States are the single most important trade partner for China, whereas the United States has another trading partner who is almost as important as China.

The discrepancy of 0,78% between the bilateral trade ratios of the United States (3,21%) and China (2,43%) would be interpreted by proponents of purely quantitative analysis as asymmetric interdependence since the United States' national income is more dependent on trade with China than the other way around (Mansfield and Pollins 2001, 847). While bilateral trade to GDP ratio is a good indicator for the level of economic interconnectedness between two states, it only has high validity for how sensitive a country is to changes in a trade relationship and has very limited validity for the level of economic vulnerability. A deterioration of economic ties between two countries whose trade makes up a notable share of both countries' GDP will result in in some level of opportunity costs but these might only be short dated and not very severe if the losses can be compensated (Mansfield and Pollins 2001, 848). Compensation for imports can be achieved through substitution by other trade partners or by increased domestic production. The loss of export opportunities can be balanced out by expanding to new markets or by stimulating domestic demand. Thus, close bilateral trade relations only result in vulnerabilities if no sufficient alternative export and import markets are available, if domestic production possibilities are too limited or unprofitable or if conditions in terms of selling prices, purchasing prices and product quality are less favourable. As laid out in chapter 2.2, sensitivity interdependence is less strong than vulnerability interdependence as it results in less opportunity costs. Consequently, the overall level of economic interdependence depends more on how vulnerable a country is to changes in trade than on the simple size of the trade volume.

The degree of dependence in a bilateral trade relationship may further vary based on the importance that the traded commodities have for each trade partner. If the majority of traded goods are non-essential like e.g. luxury goods the dependence on bilateral trade relations will be far less distinct as if trade would be primarily made up of high-technology goods[1];even though the total trade volume can still be relatively high because of the monetary value of luxury goods (Reuveny and Kang 1998, 583–84).

---

1   For this reason the wide-spread argument that economic interdependence was very high among European countries before World War One is highly debatable because luxury goods and other non-strategic goods made up a large share of trade (Blanchard and Ripsman 1996)

Therefore, it is necessary to know the composition of trade and the trade flow directions in terms of imports and exports in order to assess the level of economic interdependence more precisely. This can only be achieved by analysing more disaggregated trade data since the simple aggregation of exports and imports in trade volume, that is used for the bilateral trade to GDP ratio, ignores too many factors which are essential to unravel what makes countries truly interdependent. However, theoretical as well as empirical research on economic interdependence so far has almost exclusively focused on total trade volumes, which is why Li and Reuveny claim that the existing literature has two aggregation biases as data is aggregated across economic sectors or commodity groups as well as across trade flow directions. While some limited work on the influence of the composition of trade on economic interdependence exists, there is a lack of studies that explore the role of trade flows and how economic interdependence may differ between imports and exports. (Li and Reuveny 2008, 1–2).

This gap in the research will be addressed in the following chapters. To determine the economic interdependence that results from bilateral trade ties more precisely imports and exports will be analysed separately for the United States and China. Special attention will be given to the composition of imports and exports in order to find out how vulnerable each country is to restrictions in Sino-American trade.

4.3 United States

4.3.1 Imports

China is by far the most important import market for the United States. The United States imported goods with a combined value of 481,5 billion US dollars from China in 2016. The number is even more impressive in relation to other US imports since imports from China made up approximately 21% of the entire US imports from around the world in 2016 (UN Comtrade 2018). This figure alone already shows that trade relations with China are essential for the United States. Compensating a loss of one fifth of imports is nearly impossible regardless of which commodities are imported. Without goods from China a lot of supermarket shelves would stay empty, countless factories would have to stop production due to insufficient supplies and the business model of US companies who outsource their production to China would come to a sudden end.

Table 9: Top 10 Import Markets for Goods in 2016

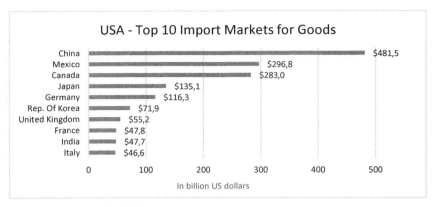

Source: (UN Comtrade 2018)

Other important trade partners have by far less relevance for the supply of goods to the US economy. Imports from its neighbouring country Mexico, which is the second largest import market for the United States, have only a total value of 296,8 billion US dollars. This is 40% less than what the United States imported from China in 2016 and only equals 13% of the value of all US imports in that year. Canada is the third largest import market with a total value of 283,0 billion US dollars which equals 12% of total US imports in 2016 (UN Comtrade 2018).

Combined imports from Mexico and Canada made up 25% of all US imports, while China alone accounted for 21%. The difference of only 4% in the total value of imports is quite remarkable given the advantages in transportation costs due to the proximity of Mexico and Canada. Imports from China must cross the Pacific Ocean and even though sea freight costs declined in recent years it is still a competitive advantage that goods from Mexico and Canada can be transported to destinations in the USA by truck or train in a few days, while cargo from China has a transit time of at least 13 days only from port to port. Inland transportation, loading, documentation, customs declaration and other handling work at the origin and at the destination usually takes another 14 days which makes a total of approximately 27 days before goods from a vendor in China arrive at a facility in the United States (China Freight Broker 2016).

Not only is transportation from Canada and Mexico cheaper and faster, but due to the North American Free Trade Agreement (NAFTA) tariffs on most goods and several non-tariff barriers have been eliminated. This makes trade between the signing countries Canada, Mexico and the United States cheaper and reduces paperwork for documentation and custom declaration duties. NAFTA even includes preferential treatment for goods that originated in other NAFTA countries which facilitates the import process as a whole (Governments of Canada / United States / Mexico 2012).

That China was still able to surpass Mexico and Canada as largest import market is an extraordinary development. So is the pace in which imports from China to the United States increased over the last 25 years. In 1991 imports from China only had a volume of 20,3 billion US dollars. Compared to the import volume of 481,5 billion US dollars in 2016 this is an increase of 2372%. The drastic increase can be explained by low production costs combined with a rapid growth of the national economy which allows China to offer enormous amounts of goods for cheap prices.

Table 10: USA - Imports in Goods from China since 1991

USA - Imports in Goods from China since 1991

In billion US dollars

Source: (UN Comtrade 2018)

As mentioned above, the sheer magnitude of imports from China already makes the United States dependent due to the inability to compensate the total amount of goods that the US economy obtains from China. However, the aggregated data of total imports is not a very precise indicator for economic dependence as it only shows that the United States have a high sensitivity dependence in terms of imports (Mansfield and Pollins 2001, 848–49).

Less aggregated data is needed to determine how vulnerable the United States is to a disruption of Chinese supplies and how high the opportunity costs would be. In order to assess the level of dependency it is essential to identify the strategic relevance of the imported goods and how much of the imports are also obtainable from other countries for a similar price and of comparable quality (Dorussen 2006, 88).

There is no general definition of strategic goods, but it is common consensus that a commodity must have some level of importance for national security to be characterised as strategic. The following analysis discusses the composition of US imports from China by disaggregating trade data into product categories. In order to determine the dependency on specific product categories it will be evaluated how important they are for the US economy in general and if they can be substituted through domestic production or via imports from third countries.

Product categories are classified in the "Harmonized Commodity Description and Coding System (HS)" since it is well-established and provides very precisely defined categories. The HS differentiates between 99 product categories which each have multiple sub-chapters. Each sub-chapter can be further broken down into very specific commodity groups. Product categories have 2-digit codes, sub-chapters have 4-digit codes and commodity groups have 6-digit codes (World Customs Organization 2018).

When US import data is disaggregated into 2-digit categories and ordered by the relevance of China as supplier it is revealed that the United States imports some goods almost exclusively from China; see table 10. Roughly 92% of all umbrellas, walking sticks and whips (HS Code 66) and 82% of all Toys, games and sports requisites (HS Code 95) that the United States imported in 2016 came from China.

Table 11: Dependence on Goods from China

Dependence on Goods from China

	66: Umbrealls, walking Sticks, whips	95: Toys, games and sports requisites	67: Feathers and down and articles thereof	65: Headgear and parts thereof	42: Articles of leather, saddlery, travel goods
	92%	82%	76%	65%	59%

US Imports from China as percentage of imports from World (all products 21%)

Source: (International Trade Center 2018; calculations based on UN Comtrade)

Importing such a high share of certain products from only one source makes the United States highly sensitive to China as a supplier of these products. It does not necessarily make the United States vulnerable if sufficient alternative suppliers are available, but the more a state relies on a single supplier, the higher is the likelihood that supplies cannot be adequately compensated by other sources. Compensation is a real challenge for the United States as for some commodities the costumer-supplier relationship between the United

States and China is close to what is called "single sourcing" in business administration.

For example, 96% of imported Umbrellas (HS Code 6601) come from China. At the same time China is the biggest exporter of umbrellas in the world with a total value of umbrella exports of 2,4 billion US dollars. This equals a market share of 82% of all exported Umbrellas in 2016. The second biggest exporter of Umbrellas is Germany with a total value of umbrella exports of 0,103 billion US dollars which equals a market share of 3,5%. The rest of the market share is divided among several other countries. Thus, there is no competitor who is even remotely at eye level with China (UN Comtrade 2018).

The US imported umbrellas with a value of 0,493 billion US dollars in 2016 which is almost five times the total exports of the second largest umbrella exporter. All umbrella exports that do not originate from China make up a total value of 0,529 billion US dollars. This is just about enough to satisfy the United States' demand but it is highly unlikely that the United States would be able to secure almost all non-Chinese umbrella exports (UN Comtrade 2018).

Another factor is the price of umbrellas from other countries. Prices per piece are not available for this product, but UN Comtrade data provides the total monetary value as well as the net weight of exported umbrellas for each country which allows calculating the price per kg. This is not a perfect indicator for price differences because the average weight of an umbrella can differ across countries, but it is close enough to allow for a meaningful comparison. Umbrellas from China cost 5,6 US dollars per kg, while German umbrellas have a price of 14,4 US dollars per kg, which makes umbrellas from Germany almost three time as expensive. The quality of Chinese umbrella's is possibly lower but most people do not carry expensive high-quality models but rather the cheap versions that can be bought at any convenient store (UN Comtrade 2018).

Consequently, it is not only close to impossible to compensate the quantity of umbrellas that are imported from China, but the alternative products are also way more expensive. If China, for any reason, would stop to export umbrellas to the United States, it would not take long until a supply shortage would occur and the umbrellas still in stock would become way more expensive due to the shortage and because of the higher purchasing price of alternative suppliers. This means that for umbrellas the United States has a very high vulnerability dependence towards China.

However, the overall importance of umbrellas for the US economy is very low since it is an everyday object and not a critical good in a supply chain or a product that has a special significance for a whole sector. Without umbrellas people would get wet when they walk in the rain, but no assembly lines would stop and except a few people who work in specialised shops nobody would lose his job. Therefore, Umbrellas are a good example of a commodity that only causes very low economic dependence even despite a very high sensitivity and vulnerability dependence since the opportunity costs of having less umbrellas are negligible. This kind of economic context is totally neglected when a study only uses aggregated data. Therefore, not considering what is traded can result in wrong assumptions which delegitimatises the validity of large-N studies.

The umbrella example shows the main weakness of assessing only the share of imports from China compared to imports from the rest of the world across product categories in order to identify how dependent the United States is from certain Chinese imports. A better indicator for the importance of a product is the monetary value of the exchanged good. The total value of all imported commodities in a product group is composed of the price per unit and the quantity of imports. Thus, product groups that have a very high share in the total value of imports either consist of very expensive commodities or are imported in vast numbers or a combination of both.

The price per unit depends on how processed or scarce the commodity is. Therefore, expensive commodities are either not so easy to produce (like a machine) or not available in great quantities (like rare raw materials). That makes the price a good indicator for the importance of a commodity. Quantity is a good indicator because it shows how high the demand for a certain commodity is and high demand means that the commodity is either very popular among consumers (like consumer electronics) or required by large parts of the local economy (like basic components in a value chain).

Imports by Product Category

When imports from China are sorted by the total monetary value of each product category it becomes clear that technical goods have a very high significance. Electronic equipment and electrical machinery (HS 85) makes up 131,7 billion out of the total 481,7 billion dollars that the US imported from China in 2016. The biggest item within the product category HS 85 are telephones and communications apparatus (HS 8517) with a value of 60,9 billion US dollars, followed by monitors and projectors (HS 8528) with 10,2 billion US dollars, electric transformers (HS 8504) with 5,6 billion US dollars and electric heaters, ovens, microwaves and other electric kitchen appliances (HS 8516) with 5,5 billion US dollars. Microchips also belong to HS 85 but are separated into the sub-chapters semi-conductor devices (HS 8541) and integrated circuits (HS 8542). Combined imports of microchips from China had a total value of 5,4 billion US dollars in 2016 (UN Comtrade 2018).

Table 12: USA - Imports from China by value of product category (HS2)

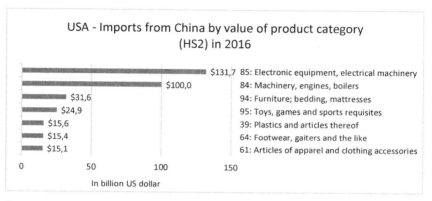

Source: (International Trade Center 2018; calculations based on UN Comtrade data)

The product category with the second highest value is also composed of technical goods like machinery, engines and boilers (HS 84). The total value of imported goods from this category amounts to 100 billion US dollars. Computers (HS 8471) make up almost half of the value with 47,4 billion US dollars. The next biggest items are parts for office machines (HS 8473) with 10,7 billion US dollars, printers (HS 8443) with 6,9 billion US dollars and valves and taps (HS 8481) with 3,4 billion US dollars (UN Comtrade 2018).

Other product categories have a considerably lower share in the total value of imports from China. Especially interesting is the gap between the second and third product category in the value ranking. Furniture, bedding and mattresses (HS 94) accounts for 31,6 billion dollars of total imports which is three times less than the value of imported machinery, engines and boilers (HS 84). The subsequent product categories make up even smaller shares and mainly consist of consumer durable goods like toys (HS 95), plastic kitchenware (HS 39), footwear (HS84) or clothing (HS 61). These products are typically designated for the end consumer market and consumed more frequently than most technical goods in categories HS 84 and HS 85. Consumer durable goods do not have a high price as they are easy to produce and available in great quantities. They still appear relatively high in the import value raking because of their high consumption rate. Clothes, footwear, toys and plastics are in high demand among American consumers, which give them some significance for US-Chinese trade relations, but just as with umbrellas the consequences of a shortage of these products are not that severe for the overall economy (UN Comtrade 2018).

However, shortages in technical goods like electronic equipment (HS 85) or machinery (HS 84) can have negative effects on large parts of an economy since several commodities in these products categories are either significant for a modern industrial society (communication technology, computers) or important components in value chains (electronic transformers, semi-conductors, integrated circuits). As illustrated in table 12, product category HS 85 makes up 27,3% of the total value of all imports and HS 84 accounts for 20,7%. Thus, almost half of what the United States spends for imports from China can be attributed to only these two product categories. This is quite remarkable given the overall amount of 99 product categories and a strong indicator that the United States is highly dependent on imports from China for commodities from product categories HS 85 and HS 84.

Table 13: US imports by product category as percentage of total value of imports from China (HS 2)

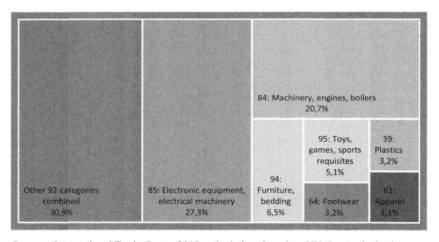

Source: (International Trade Center 2018; calculations based on UN Comtrade data)

When the import volume of other suppliers for commodities from categories HS 85 and HS 84 is compared to the import volume from China it becomes even more obvious how dependent the United States is on electronic equipment and machinery from China. The United States purchases 39,2% of all telephones, monitors, electric transformers, and microchips (HS 58) from China. The second main source for these commodities is Mexico, which accounts for 18,5% of imports. This is less than half of the Chinese supplies and even combined with imports from Malaysia, Japan and Korea, who are the other main suppliers for product category HS 58, the import volume is still smaller than what China supplies.

Table 14: USA - Top 5 Import Markets for HS 85 (Electronic Equipment, Electrical Machinery)

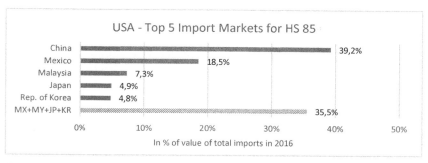

Source: (UN Comtrade 2018)

China is also by far the most important supplier for machinery, engines, and boilers (HS 84). The United States imports 31,7% of commodities from this category from China. Here, too, Mexico is the main competitor to China and accounts for 16,2% of imports in product category HS 84. This is just slightly more than half of the Chinese supplies. However, the next three largest suppliers have higher shares of total imports compared to product category HS 85 so that their combined supplies exceed the Chinese market share.

Table 15: USA - Top 5 Import Markets for HS 84 (Machinery, Engines, Boilers)

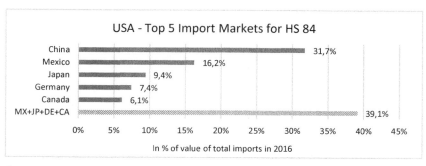

Source: (UN Comtrade 2018)

The fact that China is the United States' key supplier for the two most valuable commodity groups gives China a unique market position. A loss of supplies for these commodities would result in opportunity costs for the United States and finding sufficient alternative suppliers for 39,2%, or 31,7% respectively, of imports for certain commodities is hard to accomplish. Especially, if alternative sources of supply are as diversified as for commodities of category HS 85. The United States would need to increase imports from a great many trade partners in order to satisfy its demand, which is more complicated than substituting the supplies from China with just a single source.

This already unfavourable constellation for the United States is aggregated by China's position as market leader for exports in product category HS 85 as well as category HS 84. China has a global market share of 24,2% of all exported electronic equipment and electrical machinery (HS 85). The second largest supplier for this product category is Hong Kong with a market share of 11,36%. However, a large share of Hong Kong's exports are in fact re-exports from China that are just shipped via Hong Kong's giant freight port. Since the influence of the central government in Beijing over the special administrative region increased significantly during the last years, it can be assumed that Hong Kong would take side with China in case of a trade dispute between China and the United States. Consequently, the United States would have no access to 35,6% of world exports for commodities of product category HS 85 should China introduce an export ban (UN Comtrade 2018).

China's market share for exports of machinery, engines and boilers (HS 84) is lower than for HS85 but still amounts to 18,3%. Germany accounts for 11,9% of exports, making it the second largest supplier for commodities of this category. Since Germany is currently only the fourth largest import market to the United States for product category HS 84, see table 14, there is some potential that imports from China could be substituted with more imports from Germany. However, in order to compensate commodities from product category HS 84 with a value of 100 billion US dollars that the United States imports from China, supplies from Germany, which amounted to 23,3 billion US dollars in 2016, would need to be increased by five times (UN Comtrade 2018). This example demonstrates by just how much imports from alternatives sources would need to be expanded to make up for the incredible amounts that are currently imported from China.

Telephones and Computers

To get an even more detailed picture of which imported commodities are most relevant to the United States and if they can be substituted, the market situation for the biggest items within product category HS 85 and HS 84 is examined more closely in the following. Imported telephones and communications apparatus (HS 8517) from China had a value of 60,9 billion US dollars, which is equivalent to 46,2% of the total value of imports from product category HS 85. The biggest item in product category HS 84 are Computers (HS 8471) with a value of 47,4 billion US dollars. Since the total value of imported commodities of product category HS 84 is roughly 100 billion US dollars, computers accounted for 47,4% of the total value (UN Comtrade

2018). It is very significant that in both categories a single product sub-chapter makes up almost half of the value. It can be reasoned that these are the commodities that really matter for the United States since they are imported on a large scale and make up a large part of total imports.

Table 16: USA - Top 5 Import Markets for HS 8517 (Telephones)

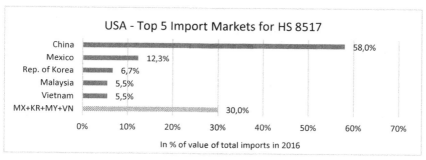

Source: (UN Comtrade 2018)

At the same time China is also the main source for both product sub-chapters. 58% of all imported telephones and other communication devices (HS 8517) come from China. China's share of imported computers is even higher and amounts to 61%. This means the United States' supply chain for these commodities is not very diversified but relies heavily on a single supplier. The market situation is far away from single sourcing but finding alternative suppliers for roughly 60% of imports is a burden. Especially, since other suppliers only account for relatively small shares of imports.

Table17: USA - Top 5 Import Markets for HS 8471 (Computers)

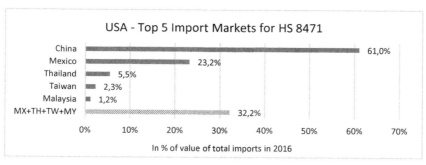

Source: (UN Comtrade 2018)

Relying heavily on a single supplier does not automatically make the United States dependent on China but where could the United States look for alternative suppliers? China is also the world export champion for both commodities and holds a market share of 40,1% of world exports in telephones and 42,3% in computers. This circumstance is aggravated by the fact that Hong Kong is one of the biggest alternative suppliers with a world export market share of 15% for telephones and 6,4% for computers of which a large share are re-exports from China; see table 18. Thus, Beijing in fact controls 55,1% of world exports in telephones and 48,7% in computers. Consequently, the United States is faced with the situation that China can take away 58% of telephone and 61% of computer imports and only 44,9% or respectively 51,3% of world supplies are available to compensate these losses since China is also the world export leader for these commodities.

Table 18: World Export Champions for HS 8517 and HS 8471

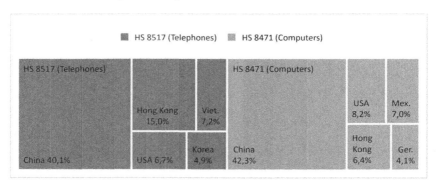

Source: (UN Comtrade 2018)

The nature of the imported goods exacerbates the dependence even more since

"manufacturing in machinery, electronics, and other high tech products relies on the general availability of highly skilled labour, and trade in these commodities is often highly asset specific." (Dorussen 2006, 98)

Asset specificity for machinery and electronics makes it even harder to find appropriate substitutes because other large suppliers of telephones or computers might not produce the specific product that the US imports from China but other kinds of telephones and computers which do not fulfil the same purpose. For example, file servers and desktop computers both belong to product sub-chapter computers (8471). China is the biggest exporter of file servers and Mexico is the biggest exporter of desktop computers. If the United States can no longer get file servers from China it does not help that it could instead get desktop computers from Mexico (UN Comtrade 2018).

However, the United States itself is also among the top exporters of telephones (6,7%) and computers (8,2%), which opens up the opportunity to compensate losses with its own production. This is a very realistic scenario as a precedent exists in which the United States introduced an export ban, namely on crude oil, in order to secure sufficient supplies for the domestic market. The export ban had been concluded in 1975 in reaction to the first oil crisis and was intended to shield the United States from global price volatilities. Export restrictions on domestically produced crude oil were only lifted in 2016 in the wake of the shale oil revolution which made the United States self-sufficient in its oil supply (Langer, Huppmann, and Holz 2016, 1).

This shows that export restrictions can be a viable measure to reduce import dependencies. The effectiveness of such measures depends on the size of domestic production that is currently exported and redirectable for domestic consumption. In 2016 the United States exported telephones worth 33,8 billion US dollars while it imported telephones from China with a total value of 60,9 billion US dollars. Exports of computers by the United States had a volume 22,3 billion US dollars in 2016 and computer imports from China amounted to 47,7 billion US dollars. Hence, the United States would be able to reduce the supply gap that China could cause to 27,1 billion US dollars for telephones and to 25,4 for computers (UN Comtrade 2018). Such an import substitution strategy would surely be accompanied with an expansion of domestic production that could even further reduce the supply gap. However, it is not possible to make a scientifically sound approximation how fast domestic production could be increased which is why this variable is not factored in.

A major problem of import substitution is that domestic production is often not competitive regarding price, quality or quantity. Most of the time the very reason to import a commodity is that somebody else can produce it at a lower price, in larger quantities or has the better product. One would assume that quality is not an issue since the United States is a high-technology country, but in an interview with Forbes Magazine Tim Cook, the CEO of Apple, pointed out that the

"U.S. is sorely lacking in certain critical skills required in the manufacturing supply chain. One of these skills is precision tooling and specifically, tooling engineers. The products we do require really advanced tooling. In the U.S. you could have a meeting of tooling engineers and I'm not sure we could fill the room. In China you could fill multiple football fields." (Forbes Magazine 2018)

A major challenge in the production of Advanced Technology Products (ATP) is to assemble large amounts of highly sophisticated machines at high quality. Over time China has built a large work force who has the necessary skills to deliver good quality in large quantities. In the United States, however, a lot of knowledge in manufacturing has been lost and it takes time to regain this knowledge and train enough workers to reach a sufficient production output.

Differences in production costs are also still an issue even though the labour costs in China have risen significantly in recent years. The price per unit for commodities of the sub-chapter telephones (HS 8517) is not available, but for commodities that are categorised as computers the price difference per unit in 2016 was 201,34 US dollars. Computers exported by the United States have been sold for an average price per unit of 283,66 US dollars, while computer exports from China had an average price per unit of 82,32 US dollars, which makes US computers 344,5% more expensive (UN Comtrade 2018).

The validity of the figures is limited since a large part of the price difference might be retraceable to a difference in what kinds of computers have been trade. It could be that the United States exported more high-end computer equipment which has a higher retail price. However, a price difference per unit of 344,5% is so high that it is reasonable to assume that production costs are responsible for a considerable part of the price difference. And even if 100% of the price difference would stem from differing product types it would mean that domestic US production could substitute none of the computer imports from China because it only produces totally different types of computers. Therefore, import substitution is not a feasible option for the United States since domestic production has either not the skills to produce the specific types of products which the United States imports from China or has not the ability to produce goods in the same quantity or cannot substitute the imported goods for a similar price.

How high the price difference would approximate be has been tested for the most prestigious American telecommunication device, the iPhone. The MIT Technology Review calculated how much an iPhone would cost if it were made entirely in the United States. Calculations are based on the price of an iPhone 6s Plus in June 2016. The components of an iPhone 6s Plus cost 231,5 US dollars and assembling all parts in China costs 4,5 US dollars which adds up to a total production cost of 236 US dollars per unit. Based on the MIT study the production of all parts in the United States would raise the component costs by at least 30-40 US dollars per unit. Extra costs for assemblage in the United States are calculated with another 30-40 US dollars per unit which results in higher costs of 60 to 80 US dollars per iPhone and total production costs of 296 to 316 US dollars. Given that Apple sells the iPhone 6s Plus for roughly three times the production costs it can be estimated that the retail price for an iPhone 6s Plus made in the United States would increase from 749 US dollars to between 939 US dollars and 1003 US dollars. Thus, an all-American iPhone would be 25% to 34% more expensive (Kakeas 2016).

Table 19: How much would an iPhone cost if it were made in the USA

Calculation for an iPhone 6s Plus in June 2016		
Country	Production Costs	Retail Price (June 2016)
Made in China	236 US dollars	749 US dollars
Made in USA	296–316 US dollars (+60-80 US dollars)	939–1003 US dollars (+190-254 US dollars)

Source: (Kakeas 2016)

Apple's iPhone is already at the top of the smart phone price range. If the retail price increases by 25% or more it is very likely that the product is not competitive any more since the price distance to comparable smartphones from Apple's competitors, who are all based in East Asia, would become enormous. Assuming that the average price increase for other domestically produced communication and computer equipment would also be in the 25% range, all US IT companies who relocate their production to the United States would lose global competitiveness. Even patriot US costumers will likely not want to or simply cannot afford to pay 25% more for the label "made in USA".

Shifting supply chains to other countries is also very difficult for Apple because only a few countries have a well enough trained work workforce and the know-how to process and assemble Advanced Technology Products. There is talk that manufacturing for some Apple product lines, mainly older version of the iPhone and the iPad, could be moved to India. India still has a demand for these cheaper Apple appliances, which is why production in India would be primarily destined for local consumption. Building up the know-how to produce the latest versions of the iPhone and realigning the supply chains would take years. Thus, Apple has no good alternatives and will be dependent on assembly centres in China for years to come (The Economist 2019b).

Rare-Earth Metals and Rare-Earth Products

A product category that is not among the imports with the highest monetary value but nonetheless crucial for the US economy are rare-earths metals and processed products that contain rare-earth metals. Rare-earth metals are a group of chemical elements that can be found in components of cell phones, computers, LEDs, flat-screen monitors, and in high-strength magnets. They also have a high military relevance because rare-earth products are used in jet engines, missile guidance systems, antimissile defence systems, satellites, and communication systems (Van Gosen, Verplanck, and Emsbo 2019, 1).

The United States sources roughly 80% of its rare-earth metal imports directly from China and rare-earth metal imports from other countries are often derived from rocks or mineral concentrates that have been extracted from Chinese deposits (U.S. Geological Survey 2019, 1). At the same time, China has a near-monopoly on rare-earth metals since 84% of the global rare-earth metal production comes from China (Van Gosen, Verplanck, and Emsbo 2019, 1). This is a very unfavourable market constellation for the United States as it comes close to single-sourcing and no sufficient alternative sources are available.

The United States has domestic rare-earth deposits and was responsible for 4% of global output but stopped mining in 2015 since domestic production was more expensive than importing rare-earth metals. Given the rising importance of rare-earth metals for the high-tech sector, the US government has issued studies to explore new rare-earth deposits as well as new extraction methods (Van Gosen, Verplanck, and Emsbo 2019, 4). However, substituting Chinese imports with domestic production is impossible because the United States' rare-earth reserves are only 3% the size of China's natural deposits (U.S. Geological Survey 2019, 2).

It must also be taken into consideration that China is the market leader for rare-earth processing and supplies the whole world with products made of rare-earth metals. China's global market share for processed rare-earth metals was as high as 95% in 2011 (Van Gosen, Verplanck, and Emsbo 2019, 4). Rare-earth magnets are the most important rare-earth products because they are used across a wide range of industries. Magnets made of rare-earth metals are essential parts of motors, rotors, generators, turbines, engines, couplings, separators, and speakers to name just a few applications (United Magnetics 2019a). 65% of the United States' rare-earth magnet imports come from Chinese producers. The next largest supplier is Japan which accounts for 11% of rare-earth magnet imports. However, Japan has no domestic rare-earth metal production which means that the raw material must be imported by Japan and Japan also sources most rare-earth metals from China. If China would cut of rare-earth exports to the United States as well as Japan, the US would be deprived of 76% of rare-earth magnet imports (UN Comtrade 2018).

Consequently, it would not be enough for the United States to find sufficient alternative suppliers for rare-earth metals to become independent from China, but it must also substitute most rare-earth product imports. This constellation creates an extraordinarily high vulnerability dependence on access to the Chinese market. A breakdown of supplies would result in high costs for the US high-tech industry and could even force businesses to shut down because many electrical and mechanical devises cannot operate without components made of rare-earths. Insufficient supply of rare-earth metals also poses a risk to the United States' national security due to the application in military technology.

Dependence on Imports

Summarising the above, this leaves the United States in the following situation:

- The majority of imports from China are Advanced Technology Products (ATP) like electronic equipment (HS 85), machinery or engines (HS 84) and not anymore low value-added products.
- The most important import items are telephones and communication devices (HS 8517) and computers (HS 8471), which are of utmost importance in today's high-technology economy. Arguably, computers and smartphones are the two key inventions of the 20th and 21st century, respectively.
- The United States' main supplier for HS 85, HS 84, HS 8471, and HS 8517 is China, which results in a very strong sensitivity dependence. Depending on the product category, China can take away between 31,7% and up to 58% of American high-technology imports.
- China is by far the leading exporter in the world for HS 58, HS 84, HS 8471, and HS 8517 with world export market shares of up to 42,3% for certain items. Therefore, it is very hard to find sufficient alternative suppliers, which causes a high vulnerability dependence.
- Domestic production of these products is not competitive in terms of price, quality, and quantity. When import substitution is not a feasible option vulnerability interdependence is even higher.

When sensitivity and vulnerability dependence for imports are high and the imported goods are not just umbrellas, but have great importance for the whole economy, then the importing country is faced with huge opportunity costs in case of a disruption of trade. The above described constellation is so unfavourable that the United States also has no chance to adapt its import strategy without suffering significant adjustment costs.

These adjustment costs get more severe, the more highly asset-specific the traded goods are. Advanced Technology Products are especially asset-specific because telephones and computers consist of thousands of components of which some are only produced in one country or even only by one company. In high-tech industries it is also not unusual that companies require customised components for which suppliers have to build specific production facilities (Fuchs 2011, 4 ff.). If only one or very few suppliers hold a specific asset, in this case specific electronic components, the buyer will suffer significant costs when he tries to find another business partner and runs the risk that he cannot get enough of the assets he needs, which could have devasting consequences if these assets are part of a supply-chain and required to continue production.

It must be pointed out that this dependence is mutual as suppliers of highly asset-specific products cannot easily find alternative buyers due to the specificity of their goods. In case of customised production, the supplier is even faced with the risk of a complete loss of his investments. That is one of the reasons why US-China trade relations are reciprocal. Chapter 4.4.1, which discusses Chinese exports to the United States, will examine this circumstance in more detail.

China's export monopoly for rare-earth metals, however, results only in a high US import dependence and does not cause mutual dependence because demand for this commodity, which is essential for high-tech supply chains, is high throughout the world and global supplies are limited. The dependence on rare-earth metals is also reflected in the decision to remove rare-earth metals and rare-earth magnets from US tariff lists that target Chinese exports to the United States (United Magnetics 2019b).

Because of the United States' high economic dependence on imports from China, a disruption of trade relations would be very expensive. Reducing the import dependence is very difficult since no sufficient alternative suppliers exist for large parts of what the United States currently source from China. Thus, the United States will remain dependent on Chinese imports for the foreseeable future and cannot avoid significant negative consequences for its economy in case China would cut shipments to the United States.

4.3.2   Exports

In terms of American exports China is not yet the most important partner country. The largest export markets for US goods in 2016 have been the neighbouring countries Canada and Mexico with a value of exported goods of 266,8 billion US dollars and 229,7 billion US dollars, respectively. Exports to China had a value of 115,6 billion US dollars in 2016 which makes it the third largest export market for the United States. While this is only half of what the United States exported to Mexico it still makes up 8% of the United States' total exports and supports around 1,5 million jobs in the domestic economy (Oxford Economics 2017, 9). Furthermore, China is by far the most important overseas market for US exports. Thus, it has a key significance as sales market for US products.

Table 20: USA - Top 10 Export Markets for Goods in 2016

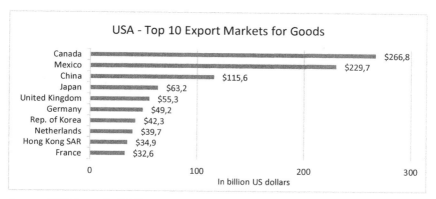

Source: (UN Comtrade 2018)

What should also be considered is the steep growth of US exports to China. In the year 2000 only 2,1% of US exports went to China. Since then the export volume increased by 705% from 16,2 billion US dollars in 2000 to 130,4 billion US dollars in 2017. This dynamic was only interrupted during the global financial crisis in 2009 and more recently when exports to China dropped from 123,7 billion US dollars in 2014 to 115,6 billion US dollars in 2016, which is a decline of 6,4% over two years.

Table 21: USA - Exports in Goods to China since 1991

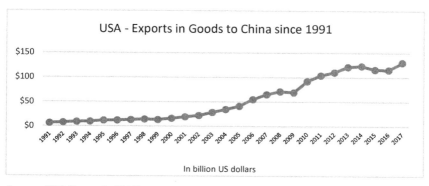

Source: (UN Comtrade 2018)

The recent drop in exports can partly be attributed to a slowing Chinese economy, but to a larger part the downturn is the result of a general decline of US exports. Globally, US exports even dropped by 10,6% between 2014 and

2016 (Morrison 2018, 3). Exports to China recovered in the following year and increased by 12,8% or in absolute numbers by 14,8 billion US dollars, thus continuing the positive trend.

Oxford Economics predicts that US exports to China will even increase faster in the near future because of China's continuing economic growth which increases the overall demand and due to rising wages that allow Chinese costumers to buy more US consumer products. According to Oxford Economics' forecast, the volume of US exports in goods to China could reach 520 billion US dollars by the year 2030, which would be roughly twice of what the United States currently exports to Canada. This means that already within the next ten years China could become the most important export market for US goods. No other sales market has this kind of growth potential and offers so many opportunities for US companies to expand their businesses. Thus, trade with China is of utmost importance for the GDP growth of the United States economy in the next decades - all the more as the saturation of most other markets, including the domestic American market, is already quite high (Oxford Economics 2017, 6).

Exports by Product Category

While the Chinese market is of high importance for most US export industries, some sectors are especially dependent on exports to China. The United States exported grain, fruits, and seeds (HS 12) worth 14,9 billion US dollars to China in 2016 which is roughly 12,8% of total US exports to China.

Table 22: USA - Exports to China by Value of Product Category (HS2) in 2016

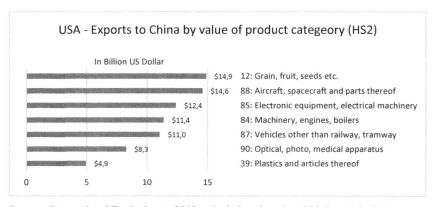

Source: (International Trade Center 2018; calculations based on UN Comtrade data)

The product category aircraft, spacecraft and parts thereof (HS 88) has the second highest export value with 14,6 billion US dollars and a share of 12,6 % of total exports to China. Other industries that have a high exposure to business with China are producers of electronic equipment (HS 85), machinery (HS 84), cars and other vehicles (HS 87) and optical, photo or medical apparatus (HS 90). All of which are key technology industries.

Soya Beans

Within the product category grain, fruit and seeds (HS 12) soya beans (HS 1201) account for 14,2 billion US dollars which is 95,3% of the total value of exports in that product category. At the same time China is also by far the single most important export market for soya beans as the United States sells 62% of its global soya bean exports to China. The four next largest buyers combined purchased only 18,5% of total US exports. Due to this extreme market constellation, it can be assumed that American producers of soya beans would not be able to find enough buyers if China would stop to import soya beans from the United States. Thus, a Chinese import stop would lead to a huge overproduction which in consequence would cause a price decline for soya beans. China can use this market power to push prices downward but would likely face supply shortages as a consequence. An easier way to hurt the American agroindustry would be to raise tariffs on soya beans in order to shrink the profits from soya bean exports. Due to the lack of alternative markets soya bean producers would find themselves compelled to accept the higher tariffs.

Table 23: USA - Top 5 Export Markets for HS 1201 (Soya Beans)

USA - Top 5 Export Markets for HS 1201 (Soya Beans)

Market	% of value of total exports in 2016
China	62,0%
Mexico	6,4%
Japan	4,4%
Indonesia	4,3%
Netherlands	3,4%
MX+JP+ID+NL	18,5%

In % of value of total exports in 2016

Source: (UN Comtrade 2018)

Aircraft

The market constellation for the second most important product category according to value of exported goods is not as extreme but China is also the main buyer of American air- and spacecraft. 10,8% of all airplanes and helicopters that US companies exported in 2016 were purchased by China. The next largest customers are France who bought 9,1% of American aircraft and the United Kingdom with 8,1%. Thus, exports in this category are more evenly distributed and other export markets have a similar importance for American aircraft exports as China. Therefore, China has less market power than in the case of soya beans but finding alternative buyers for 10,8% of exports is still not easy. Especially, considering that airplanes and helicopters are not daily consumer goods but highly asset-specific products.

Table 24: USA - Top 5 Export Markets for HS 88 (Aircraft, Spacecraft)

USA - Top 5 Export Markets for HS 88

Market	%
China	10,8%
France	9,1%
United Kingdom	8,1%
Japan	5,9%
Canada	5,6%
CA+JP+GB+FR	28,7%

In % of value of total exports in 2016

Source: (UN Comtrade 2018)

Airplanes and helicopters are normally not produced on stock but on customer order basis. Product lines like the Airbus A380 or the Boeing 747 allow for a standardised production but in most cases the airplane models are modified according to customer requirements. Some airlines want more seats in the first class while others do not even offer a first class anymore. Leg space between seat rows and entertainment systems are other examples of features that can vary from order to order. Thus, airplanes cannot easily be resold if a customer withdraws his order. This makes the production of airplanes asset-specific.

The financial risk that comes along with asset specificity is especially high for very large orders which require to hire new employees, expand production facilities or even to build new factories. A good example is the Airbus factory in Tianjin which has been expanded after China ordered 75 Airbus A330 for its national airlines in 2015 (Aerotelegraph 2015). The US competitor Boeing even started to build a completely new overseas factory in

Zhoushan in 2017. The decision to move parts of the final assembly to China is not connected to any particular order but was only motivated by a good business outlook (Xinhua News Agency 2017). Boeing sold more than 200 planes to China in 2016 which makes it the largest export market for Boeing. Already one in every four Boeing airplanes is exported to China. Only at home in the United States the company is even more successful (UN Comtrade 2018; Aero 2018). For the next 20 years from 2017 until 2036 Boeing predicts that China will need 7240 new planes with a market value of 1,1 trillion US dollars (Boeing 2017, 32). If the forecast is accurate and if Boeing secures orders for a large portion of the new planes, the factory in China will definitively pay off. But if the numbers fall short of expectation or if competitors are getting the lion's share of the estimated 1,1 trillion US dollars orders then Boeing's investment in China could become a loss-making business.

Joint Ventures

Boeing is not the only US company who relies heavily on China and made major investments. General Motors has 11 joint ventures with Chinese companies who produce most of GM's vehicle line for the Chinese market. Already since 2010 GM sells more cars in China than in the United States. In 2016 a total of 3,87 million cars have been sold by GM in China whereas sales in the United States only reached around 3 million cars. A large share of these sales does not appear in the US export data because GM's joint ventures produce on-site in China and only a small number of cars is still exported from the United States. However, GM makes huge profits with this business model which eventually benefits the US economy and secures jobs in the Detroit company headquarters. In 2016 the equity income from GM's joint venture operations in China was 2 billion US dollars (General Motors 2017, 3 ff.). As sales figures rose steadily over the last years it is very likely that the Chinese market will become even more important for GM. In 2016 General Motors sold 7,1% more cars in China than in 2015 and since the Chinese vehicle market is forecast to increase by another 5 million cars until 2020, there is still a great deal of potential for further growth (General Motors 2016). No other market is offering this potential which is why continued access to the Chinese market is essential for the business success of General Motors.

In many industry sectors joint ventures with local Chinese companies are a prerequisite for foreign companies to set up business in China. Apart from GM and the other two major US car manufacturers Ford and Chrysler also big restaurant companies like Pizza Hut, Taco Bell and KFC (all YUM Brands Inc.) or McDonalds and Starbucks have entered joint ventures to open branches in China. Sino-American joint ventures are also common in the telecommunication sector, in tourism or in the insurance industry. US companies involved in this business model do not get income from exports but from their shareholdings in Chinese offshoot companies. And joint ventures are not the only way to make money in China. Licence fees are a huge source of income for American companies who do business in China. Therefore, export figures alone are not a good indicator for the importance of China for US businesses.

US Corporate Revenue Exposure to China

How much revenue American companies make in China tells more about how dependent the US economy is on economic relations with China than the volume of exports. Revenue can either be acquired via sales, equity income or licensing fees, which means that export earnings are included in revenue numbers. When American companies are ranked by their revenue exposure to China it becomes obvious that especially IT companies who produce semiconductors (HS 8541) or integrated circuits (HS 8542) rely heavily on the Chinese market. 12 out of the 15 companies with the highest revenue exposure to China belong to the microchip sector. The semi-conductor producer Skyworks Solutions generates as much as 83% of its global revenue from business in the Chinese market.

Table 25: US Companies with Highest Revenue Exposure to China in 2014

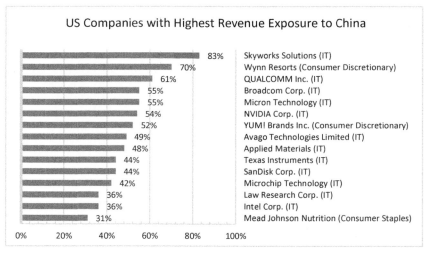

Source: (Goldman Sachs Global Investment Research 2015)

Four other chip manufacturers (Qualcomm, Broadcom, Micron Technology and Nvidia) make more than 50% of their earnings in China. While Skyworks Solutions makes almost all of its money with hardware sales, companies like Qualcomm get a large share of their revenue from licensing fees for microchips that are produced by Chinese companies who use the blueprints and patents of the US company (Goldman Sachs Global Investment Research 2015).

Since a revenue exposure of 83% to a single market is remarkably high, it is worth taking a closer look at the business model of Skyworks solutions. The company has specialised in the production of semi-conductors that enable wireless communication like Wi-Fi switches, antenna tuner, Bluetooth modules or power amplifiers. Its products are used in mobile phones, tablets, cellular and radio network systems, cars, medical devises and also in military equipment. Skyworks supplies all major Chinese consumer electronics and mobile communication companies like Huawei, Oppo Electronics, Vivo Communication Technology or Xiaomi Tech. Of these four companies Huawei is the only one who is well established outside of China, but due to the size of the Chinese market the other three still belong to the ten biggest mobile phone manufacturers in the world (Skyworks 2018a).

In Huawei's flagship mobile phone Mate 10 Pro a total of seven components from Skyworks are integrated. This is a high number of components considering that Skyworks only produces semi-conductors for mobile communication, i.e. LTE, WLAN or Bluetooth, and not for any other applications. The combined value of the seven components in the Mate 10 Pro is more than 10 dollars according to Skyworks, which is a significant revenue per unit (Skyworks 2018a, 10). Huawei sold 132,8 million mobile phones in 2016 which made it the third largest company in this business sector behind Samsung and Apple (Gartner 2017). If Skyworks would make 10 US dollars with every Huawei phone then the revenue from this one Chinese business partner would have been 1,328 billion US dollars in 2016 which is more than one third of Skyworks' total revenue of 3,3 billion US dollars in 2016 (Skyworks 2016, 125). Probably Skyworks makes less than 10 US dollars with cheaper Huawei models, but the calculation still shows how important this costumer is for global sales.

Another big Chinese costumer is the telecommunication corporation China Mobile. Skyworks sells semi-conductors for telephone and mobile internet antenna to China Mobile (Skyworks 2018a, 14). As the largest communication cooperation in the world China Mobile operates a huge mobile phone network that offers enormous sales opportunities for Skyworks' products. Especially since China Mobile is investing heavily in new infrastructure for faster mobile internet which means that thousands of new mobile internet antenna will be needed in the next years (PwC 2017, 52).

Skyworks' good business ties with Chinese information technology companies explain parts of its revenue exposure to China. Another reason why Skyworks makes so much money on the Chinese market is that they are a key supplier for iPhones. While Apple is an American company based in California, none of the production steps for an iPhone are conducted in the United States. Suppliers like Skyworks manufacture the components and ship them from all over the world to China for final assembly. For many years just one company, the Foxconn Technology Group, assembled every single iPhones (Xing and Detert 2010, 3). Foxconn is still the biggest iPhone assembler but two other companies, Pegatron Corporation and Wistron Corporation, have taken over the assembly for some iPhone product lines. All three companies are based in Taiwan but their factories are located in Mainland China (Apple 2018b). Foxconn is running a complex of more than 10 factories in the Shenzhen area and employs more than 100.000 people only at this one location. The total number of employees worldwide, of which a vast majority is located in Mainland China, is approximately 1,3 billion (Foxconn 2016). Skyworks' semi-conductors are integrated into millions of iPhone in these factories which is why the revenue comes from China and not from the United States.

The newest iPhone product lines are important sources of revenue for Skyworks. The iPhone 8 features a total of 19 microchips from ten different chip manufacturers. Four of them are supplied by Skyworks which is a share of 21%, whereas most other companies only contribute a single chip (iFixit 2017a). The iPhone X is equipped with 23 microchips from eleven different chip manufacturers. Skyworks also contributes four chips to the iPhone X which is equivalent to 17% of integrated chips. No other manufacturer contributes more chips to the iPhone 8 or the iPhone X. (iFixit 2017b).

The microchips that Skyworks sends to Foxconn, China Mobile, Huawei and its other Chinese partners will appear in US exports statistics as long as they have been shipped from the United States to China. However, Skyworks has shifted parts of its production to foreign countries. The company still runs three production facilities in the United States but also produces in Mexico, Japan, and Singapore. Every microchip that is produced in a factory outside the United States and shipped to China does not count towards the export volume of the United States even though factories belong to an American company. Skyworks does not publish how much of the semi-conductors that are sold to China are produced outside the United States but the value of the company's assets (i.e. property, plant and equipment) in the United States compared to the assets in foreign countries allows making an estimation about how large the production facilities in every location are. Skyworks' assets in the United States are worth 140,5 million US dollars, while assets in Mexico (355,9 million US dollars), Singapore (180,1 million US dollars) and Japan (121,6 million US dollars) add up to 657,6 million US dollars. Since company assets outside the United States are 4,7 times higher it can be concluded that foreign factories are larger and produce the majority of Skyworks' microchips (Skyworks 2016, 123). Consequently, there is a large discrepancy between US exports statistics and what Skyworks really sells to China. This is a problem since it leads to wrong interpretations of export data. After all revenue from production facilities outside the United States supports jobs at home. Apart from the headquarter in Massachusetts where the administration, sales and marketing units are located Skyworks runs design centres and engineering hubs in California, Iowa, New Jersey and North Carolina (Skyworks 2018b). Therefore, the United States economy profits way more from Skyworks business ties with China than trade statistics show.

Skyworks is no isolated case as many US companies with strong business ties to China have production facilities in foreign countries. Qualcomm Inc. is a leading chip manufacturer based in San Diego who has a revenue exposure to China of 61%. The company has production facilities in the United States but also in Germany, China and Singapore (Qualcomm 2017, 37). This means that as in the case of Skyworks a large share of Qualcomm's sales to China is not represented in US export statistics because they are not shipped from the United States. What is special about Qualcomm is that it makes roughly 29% of its revenue with licence fees on patents that are used for manufacturing of chipsets or with royalties on sales of products incorporating its intellectual property (Qualcomm 2017, 29). A total of 65% of Qualcomm's revenue from licence fees and royalties originates from Chinese licensees (Qualcomm 2017, 16). However, licence fees and royalties are classified as services and thus not recorded in merchandise trade statistics. Therefore, none of the revenue from these businesses activities is included in the US-China merchandise trade balance. As bilateral trade is usually only analysed in terms of how many goods have been exchanged between the territories of two states and not in terms of exchanged services or company revenue, the extent of US business activities in China is underestimated in most studies.

Dependence on Exports

When all American business activities with China and in China are gathered and examined, the following conclusion can be made:

- China is the third most important sales market for US products and offers the highest growth potential for further expansion of American exports. If exports continue to grow on the same level, China will become the most important export market for the United States by 2030 at the latest.
- Major exports to China are grain, fruit and seeds (HS 12), aircraft and spacecraft (HS 88), electronic equipment (HS 85), machinery and engines (HS 84) and vehicles (HS 87). Except for grain, fruit and seeds these

product categories are highly asset-specific because they require high investments in production facilities and product lines.

- Since China is the main costumer for these product categories, the sensitivity dependence on sales to China is high. In the case of Soya (HS12101) as much as 62% of exports go to China. For other product categories about 10% of American global exports are shipped to China.
- Finding alternative costumers for US products is difficult if the sensitivity dependence is as high as 62% or very costly in case of asset-specific products which require customer specific investments. Therefore, a great number of American companies who export to China have a high vulnerability dependence.
- The vulnerability dependence in form of revenue exposure is even higher than exports alone since many American companies with strong business ties to China have important alternative sources of income from their China operations. Depending on the economic sector a large part of revenue comes from joint ventures, licensing, or sales from factories outside the United States; all of which are not recorded in traditional trade data.

As sensitivity and vulnerability dependence for exports to China are high, the United States would suffer significant costs if access to the Chinese market would be restricted. The business model of whole sectors like the soya bean or computer chip industry relies on exports to China. For these sectors already the introduction of higher tariffs, which is a rather soft policy tool compared to e.g. an import ban, would have devastating consequences. The president of the American Soybean Association stated in April 2018 before the Committee on Ways and Means of the US House of Representatives that

"if China chooses to impose a 25 percent tariff [...] total U.S. soy exports would drop by 37%, and U.S. soybean production would decline by 15%." (US House of Representatives 2018, 2)

While in general agriculture has a rather low economic significance for industrialised countries, the soya bean industry in the United States is so huge that it actually is of considerable relevance; especially for the major soya bean producing US states Iowa, Minnesota, Nebraska, North Dakota and Indiana. A majority of US soya bean production is dedicated for export and contributed 27 billion US dollars to US exports in 2017 (US House of Representatives 2018, 1). This is a share of about 1,86% of total US exports in 2017 which amounted to 1450 billion US dollars (UN Comtrade 2018). Researchers from the Agricultural Economics Department at the Purdue University in Indiana have developed a model to calculate the long term negative economic effect of Chinese tariffs on the American soya bean industry. They calculate that even after an adaptation phase of 5 years a 25% tariff would still result in yearly economic losses of 3,1 billion US dollars (Hurt, Tyner, and Taheripour 2018, 4–5). Economic losses of this size paired with the aforementioned production decline of 15% would threaten many jobs in an industry that employs as much worker (~300.000) as the American steel and aluminium industry combined (~301.000) (American Soybean Association 2018).

The soya bean example shows that already small political disruptions between the United States and China, which are accompanied by trade restrictions for sectors of mediocre economic relevance, result in extensive ripple effects for American exports. Other sectors like the aircraft and microchip industry who have high investments in China would suffer even more if China would introduce restrictive measure. The Chinese government has already proven that it has no scruples about taking action against US companies in these key sectors. Qualcomm was the target of a Chinese anti-trust probe in 2013 which resulted in a 975 million dollars fine and a forced liberalizations of Qualcomm's license business in China. Business insiders claim that the probe was politically motivated and designed to decrease the dependence of Chinese smartphone manufacturers on US patents (Swanson and Stevensen 2018).

With legal measure like these it is very easy for the Chinese government to make it harder for US companies to do business in China. Unlike in the United States were companies enjoy a high level of legal certainty the Chinese one-party system facilitates government interference in business affairs of foreign companies.

Consumer boycotts are another way for Beijing to hurt US companies. When Chinese costumers boycotted Japanese products following a flare up of the Senkaku/Diaoyu islands dispute, sales of Japanese companies suffered a serious decline. Japanese car manufacturers exported 32.3% less cars to China within the following 12 months. In total Japan's exports to China declined by 2,69% within one year (Heilmann 2016, 185–86). The consumer boycotts were prompted by a series of public anti-Japanese protests that featured looting of Japanese shops and factories. The Chinese government was criticised for tolerating the protests at first, thus facilitating anti-Japanese sentiments (New York Times 2012). Given Beijing's control over the press and social media, it would be easy to encourage public anti-American protests and boycotts of US products. Western media outlets already speculate that Beijing could use consumer boycotts of apple products as leverage in trade negations (The Economist 2019b). China is one of apple's most important markets with sales amounting to 48,5 billion US dollars in 2016 and a revenue exposure of 22,5%. (Apple 2017, 23).

Thanks to China's political system the Chinese policy toolbox in a trade war with the United States is larger and allows China to target American companies more quickly and more directly. The United States would be ill-advised to engage in a trade dispute with a country who has high retaliatory capabilities which are very likely to be devastating for American exports because of the high economic vulnerability dependence of key sectors of the United States' economy.

4.3.3   US Trade Balance with China

A direct comparison of the total monetary value of US imports from and exports to China shows that the United States imports much more goods from China than it exports. Consequently, the United States has a negative trade balance with China. However, as already discussed in the last chapter, trade balance in terms of exchanged goods between two economic territories is not a very meaningful measure for commercial success anymore and can even be misleading. According to a joint report on measures of international trade by the OECD and the WTO,

"what you do - the activities a firm or country is involved in - matters more for growth and employment than what you sell - the products that make up final sales or exports." (OECD and WTO 2015b, 1)

Therefore, other dimensions of economic interaction will also be considered in this chapter to determine which trade partner benefits more from economic cooperation. However, the starting point for the analysis will be the US trade deficit in goods as this is the basis for all discussions about the asymmetry of Sino-American trade relations. No other indicator has been cited more often in journal articles, newspapers stories or political speeches on the relationship between the United States and the People's Republic of China. Reasons for that might be that trade balance in goods is easy to understand and easy to illustrate in form of a bar or graph. Another reason for the prominence of this indicator could be that the numbers are kind of "flashy" since the deficit reached an enormous size. Over the last decade the United States' negative trade balance with China grew steadily from 251 billion US dollars in 2006 to 366 billion US dollars in 2016. Such incredibly high numbers are very likely to attract attention and convey a very strong message: the United States is on the losing end of the economic relationship. While the indicator illustrates very well just how much more goods are shipped from China to the United States than the other way around, it conceals relevant information at the same time. For instance, it does not show that both, the United States imports and exports, have grown over the last decade. Thus, the increase of the deficit is not the result of declining US exports but is attributable to faster growing imports. It is important to point this out since it shows that while China might have benefitted more in this particular dimension of economic exchange, the United States' economy profited as well and expanded sales in the Chinese market considerably.

Table 26: US Trade Balance in Goods with China

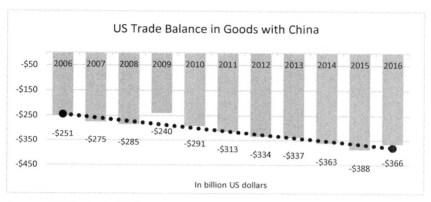

Source: (UN Comtrade 2018)

In contrast to the long-term trend, the American trade deficit decreased two times between 2006 and 2016. As illustrated in the table above the deficit decreased by 45 billion US dollars from 2008 to 2009. This drop coincides with the height of the financial crisis after the collapse of the investment bank Lehmann Brothers in September 2008. In the wake of the crisis the global trade volume decreased which is very likely the cause for the shrinking deficit. More interesting is the decrease of 22 billion US dollars from 2015 to 2016. This reduction of the gap between imports and exports is attributable to a drop in US imports from 504 billion US dollar in 2015 to 481,5 billion US dollars in 2016, whereas US exports to China remained almost unchanged (UN Comtrade 2018). Importing 22,5 billion US dollars less from one year to the next is a considerable decrease, but 481,5 billion US dollars of imported goods in 2016 is still an incredible high amount.

However, this number has to be put into perspective since imports from China have a foreign content share of 32,2%. This means that around one third of the value of China's global exports was foreign made and imported to China. When an economy is using a large number of parts and other input from foreign sources this is a strong indicator that many of its domestic companies do not manufacture a complete product but are only involved in some of the production steps. Consequently, not the complete value of goods which leave Chinese factories can be attributed to China (OECD and WTO 2015a). However, trade statistics do not differentiate between processed goods which include foreign content and completely domestically-made goods. When the United States imports something from China then the entire value of the product is ascribed to China no matter how many components are of foreign origin (Xing 2014, 115–16).

Since an increasing number of companies produce along global value chains, the practice of attributing the full value of a final product to the country who ships the finished product is outdated and leads to wrong conclusions. The export volume of countries at the end of global value chains who specialise on assemblage is inflated by traditional trade statistics which results in distorted trade balances with destination countries.

While China climbed up on the global value chain in recent years, it still plays the role of "great assembler" in many industries as illustrated by the foreign content share of 32,2% in exported goods. The share of foreign content in exported electronic equipment and electrical machinery (HS 85) is even higher and amounts to 53,8% (Morrison 2018, 13). Since electronic equipment makes up 27,3% of all US imports from China, the influence of foreign content on the US trade balance with China is significant and leads to an overestimation of the deficit.

The iPhone is a good example for a product of this category which heavily inflates the US trade deficit. Apple has diversified its supply network in recent years, but iPhones are still assembled exclusively in China. Consequently, every iPhone that is shipped to the United States counts as import from China and contributes to the trade deficit. This is strange enough since Apple is an American company and it is counterintuitive that a product from an American company appears on the negative side of the trade balance with China. While counterintuitive, this practice would be correct if the entire value of an iPhone would be created in China, but in fact only a small part of the value is added in China. In a study from 2010 the Asian Development Bank Institute calculated that only 3,6% of the value of an iPhone can be attributed to China. The rest of the value added comes from parts that China imported from supplier firms from Japan, Germany, South Korea and even the United States (Xing and Detert 2010, 5). While the share in value added has changed in the meantime as more and more high-tech components are also produced in China, it still remains a fact that iPhones are not actually made in China but manufactured along a global value chain of which China is only a part. Nevertheless, the full value of an iPhone shipped to the United States is attributed to China. In 2009 iPhones contributed 1,9 billion US dollars to the trade deficit, which was equivalent to about 0,8% of the entire deficit in that year. If only the value that is added in China would be considered in trade statistics the contribution of the iPhone to the trade deficit in 2009 would have been merely 73 million US dollars instead (Xing and Detert 2010, 5–6). This enormous difference illustrates how much global supply and value chains have changed the meaning of international trade statistics.

The example also shows that importing more than exporting is not necessarily a disadvantage for an economy. By outsourcing the production to suppliers in foreign countries Apple can reduce the production costs of an iPhone and increases the profit margin considerably. The extra revenue from the higher margin allows Apple to expand and benefits the US economy. Costumers in the United States also profit directly from outsourcing as long as a reduction in production costs results in lower retails prices.

The iPhone is not the only product which artificially inflates the US trade deficit. The value added to other Chinese high-technology exports is similarly low. Data from 2010 shows that only 3% of the total value of laptops made in China can actually be attributed to manufacturing and assembly that occurred in China. Most of the value of the finished product comes from imported components. According to international trade statistics China exported laptops with a value of 52,5 billion US dollars in 2010, while the actual value added that can be attributed to China was just about 1,6 billion US dollars (Xing 2014). Laptops belong to HS 84 (machinery, engines, and boilers) and are one of the biggest US imports from China[2] which means that this product has a considerable weight in the bilateral trade balance. Once more it must be pointed out that the value added data is from 2010. China has climbed up on the global value chain in the meantime and is not anymore at the lowest end of the value-added stage, but the attribution of the full value of an exported laptop to China is still greatly distorting trade statistics.

Globalisation and the advance of production along global value chains has made traditional methods of measuring trade balances somewhat obsolete. This is especially true for countries who export or import high quantities of Advanced Technology Products which are rarely designed, manufactured, and assembled in the same country. Today, a value added approach of measuring trade balances is needed to account for the high foreign content share in most merchandise products.

In recent years, several projects have been launched who develop data bases for trade in value added. The accuracy of value added trade statistics is already quite good, but some methodological issues still have to be solved. The main challenge is to construct accurate input-output tables which capture the share of trade in intermediate and final goods. Designing input-output tables requires the disaggregation of global trade data in order to determine which exports are designated for further processing and which are intended for consumption. However, establishing a clear link between an exported good and its utilization in the importing country is not always possible which is why estimations based on the type of the traded goods and the industry sector are used (OECD and WTO 2012, 12).

While statistics of trade in value added have some statistical impreciseness, they still give a more accurate view of international trade than traditional trade statistics since they distinguish between the total value of a product

2   See chapter 4.3.1; the total value of imported goods from category HS 84 amounts to 100 billion US dollars. Computers and Laptops (HS 8471) have a share of 47,4 billion US dollars.

and what the exporting country has added to this product in value. A bilateral balance based on value-added data can show how much of US imports from China are really of Chinese origin. The other way around it also shows how much of Chinese imports from the United States are produced in a third country. Since the foreign content share of US exports is only at about 15 % compared to 32,2% for Chinese exports, the United States trade deficit in value added is way lower than in traditional statistics.

Among the projects who construct value-added data the OECD/WTO imitative "Made in the World" is already very well established and has detailed statistics on US-China bilateral trade. According to the OECD/WTO calculation from 2011 the US trade deficit with China is in fact one third smaller when value added is accounted for (OECD and WTO 2015a, 1). Using input-output tables from the "Global Trade Analysis Project" Johnson and Noguera come to a similar result in a study from 2012. They calculate that the deficit is 30-40% smaller compared to traditional trade statistics which only measure gross exchange (Johnson and Noguera 2012, 233). More up to date value-added trade data is not available but if it is assumed that accounting for value added shrinks the trade deficit with China by 35% then the US deficit in 2016 would not have been 366 billion US dollar but 238 billion US dollar.

Table 27: US Trade Balance in Goods with China in 2016

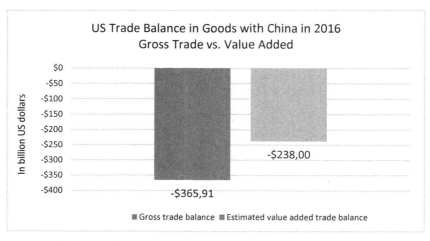

Source: Projection based on (OECD and WTO 2015a)

While being a more accurate indicator, the value added trade balance is still not telling the whole truth about who benefits more from Sino-American economic exchange. Additionally, it must be taken into consideration that most of the factories in which top export goods like mobile phones and computers are assembled do not belong to Chinese companies. Therefore, it is questionable if the value that is added to export goods by processing or assemblage can be fully attributed to China. The rise of China to become the leading exporter for Advanced Technology Products is based on the relocation of production facilities by foreign firms. Taiwanese information technology companies have outsourced 93% of their production to Mainland China. The largest assemblage facilities in China are run by Foxconn, Pegatron and Wistron which are all based in Taiwan (Morrison 2018, 12). Therefore, much of the revenue from these production steps does not stay in China, which means that China does not profit as much from high-tech exports to the United States as trade statistics imply.

Other Asian countries have also shifted production to China and not only for Advanced Technology Products. In 1990 only 3,6% of US imports came from China and 43,5% from other Asian and Pacific countries. In 2016 US imports from China and from other Asian and Pacific countries both made up roughly 21% of total US imports. This means that many products which used to be made in Japan, South Korea, Singapore or Hong-Hong are now either manufactured in China or at least assembled in China. (Morrison 2018, 11).

Table 28: USA - Imports in Goods from China and Japan

Source: (UN Comtrade 2018)

Until the year 2001 the United States imported more goods from Japan than from China and also had the largest trade deficit with Japan. But in 2002 China took over from Japan as most important import market for the United States. The table below shows that China's share of total US imports grew steadily over the last two decades while Japan became a less important source of imports in inversed proportion. This negative correlation implies that the relocation of manufacturing from Japan to China contributed heavily to the rapid increase of US imports from China and by doing so boosted the US trade deficit with China (Morrison 2018, 12). Consequently, parts of the US trade deficit with China are redirected deficits with other countries. This is another reason why bilateral trade statistic should be seen in a global context.

The incredible high amount of imports from China is the main driver of the US trade deficit with China, but as shown above traditional trade statistics point a distorted picture of the reality. US imports from China are in fact about one third smaller because of the high share of foreign content in Chinese exports. Furthermore, a large share of the rising imports from China are not additional but redirected imports because a great deal of production shifted from third countries to China. Without these shifts the United States would have higher deficits with many other Asian countries instead.

While more manufacturing is now taking place in China, the key companies in export-oriented industries are predominantly foreign-owned firms or foreign-invested firms (Xing 2014, 120). Therefore, China profits way less from exports to the United States than statistics suggest and it is very much debatable "how much China" there really is in US imports from China. Taken together, these factors lead to a massive overestimation of US imports from China.

And it is not just the overestimation of imports alone that inflates the trade deficit. At the same time US exports to China are also underestimated. The sales of foreign affiliates of American firms in China, that is business enterprises in China in which a US entity owns or controls 10% or more of the voting securities or an equivalent interest in unincorporated enterprises, have amounted to 481 billion US dollar in 2015. The sales of majority-owned foreign affiliates of American firms, that is enterprises in which a US entity owns more than 50% of voting securities, have amounted to 355 billion US dollar in 2015. As US companies receive at least 50% of the sales revenue from majority-owned foreign affiliates, they made at least 177,5 billion US dollar of revenue from investments in China (BEA 2017, 11–13). The revenue from these joint-venture activities is not accounted for in trade statistics.

What is also not considered in US exports to China is that most US companies shifted a considerable part of their production to foreign countries. This has a huge effect on the trade balance since the International Merchandise Trade Statistics guidelines define exports as the total physical movement of goods that leave the economic territory of a country (UN Trade Statistics 1998, 7). From this definition follows that if a US company has production facilities outside the United States and ships its products directly to foreign trade partners, these exports are not attributed to the United States' exports but to those country's exports in which the production facility is located. A good example for how the focus on economic territory leads to an underestimation of US exports is the semi-conductor manufacturer Skyworks Solutions who made a 2,3 billion revenue with sales to China in 2016. As mentioned in the chapter "USA – Exports of Goods", Skyworks still has three production facilities in the United States but the majority of semi-conductors are manufactured outside the United States in Mexico, Japan and Singapore (Skyworks 2016, 125). Consequently, only an inferior share of the 2,3 billion in goods that Skyworks shipped to China in 2016 are added to the sum of US exports to China.

As outsourcing production is a long-term trend across economic sectors in the United States, export figures are suffering from production abroad for a long time already. This phenomenon is not limited to exports to China but to US exports in general. As early as 1989 the New York Times highlighted this issue in an article titled "Spread of U.S. Plants Abroad Is Slowing Exports" (New York Times 1989). The description of the development from three decades ago reads like an account from today:

"In the great race for overseas sales, many American companies are rushing to manufacture abroad, finding this strategy more efficient and profitable than exporting their products from the United States. [...] The trend to locating overseas may be good for business, but it has ominous implications for the trade deficit." (New York Times Uchitell 1989)

The quote stresses that the practice to outsource manufacturing was initialised by US companies for economic reasons. This is important to point out since often trading partners are blamed for the exodus of production. While China is rightfully criticised for the joint venture requirements which force foreign companies to establish subsidiaries in cooperation with Chinese companies if they want to have full market access, this has not started the trend of relocating production centres. China was not even an important trading partner in 1989.

While the extent to which companies outsourced production to foreign countries was still relatively small in comparison to today, the article already predicted that this development would have very negative effects on the United States trade balance. But at the same time it was also pointed out that trade deficits which result from increased overseas activities do not have to be negative for the United States, since the United States economy benefits from the business success of US companies in foreign markets.

"Profits from overseas operations keep rising. If this trend continues, these earnings will eventually be counted as income for the nation." (New York Times Uchitell 1989)

The prediction from 1989 has become reality as today many US companies make more money abroad than with exports. Some companies do not even produce any physical goods in the United States anymore. Apple for example made 48,5 billion in revenue from China in 2016, which is 22,5% of its global sales, without exporting a single iPhone as assemblage takes place in China. This revenue was generated by Apple subsidiaries who handle sales and distribution for Mainland China, Hong Kong, Macau and Taiwan (Apple 2017, 23). While a large part of this money was probably not repatriated to avoid US corporate tax, it still entered the US current account as so called reinvested earnings. The term reinvested earnings is somewhat misleading as it does not mean that all of the earnings are actually spend but rather that the earnings stay "invested" in overseas activities. US companies can at any time repatriate reinvested earnings at which point the US economy and the United States budget profit from overseas earnings. That money from overseas operations actually is benefitting the home economy is demonstrated by Apple's announcement in January 2018 to repatriate almost all of its 252 billion US dollar offshore holdings. A large share of these holdings comes from business activities in China. According to the announcement, the tax revenue from the repatriation will amount to 38 billion US dollar. Apples says that it wants to use the money for investments in new data centres and a new campus, thereby creating up to 20.000 new jobs over the next five year (Apple 2018a).

Although earnings from overseas activities make up an ever larger part of US companies' revenue and enables companies to grow globally as well as at home, this component of global economic interaction is hardly ever taken into account in the public discourse on the advantages and disadvantages of international trade. Most politicians in the United States focus only on the balance of trade in terms of exchanged goods between two economic territories. This is a problem because thereby the narrative is established that only China profits from economic exchange with the United States. For example, Donald Trump accused China of "taking out massive amounts of money and wealth from the U.S. in totally one-sided trade" (Trump 2017). His assessment that trade with China is unfair and even leads to net losses for the United States, although there is evidence that trade ties with China actually support GDP growth in the United States (Oxford Economics 2017, 8), is based on the trade deficit in exchanged goods as this quote shows:

We are not in a trade war with China, that war was lost many years ago by the foolish, or incompetent, people who represented the U.S. Now we have a Trade Deficit of U.S500 Billion a year. (Trump 2018a)

It must be pointed out that the United States' trade deficit with China never was as high as 500 billion US dollar. The deficit in 2017 amounted to 375,5 billion US dollar according to the United States Census Bureau (United States Census Bureau 2019); a source that Donald Trump quoted himself in the past (Trump 2014). US Imports from China had a total volume of 505 billion US Dollar in 2017, which is likely the number the president referred to in his post on Twitter. That the president only looks at how much money Americans have paid for Chinese goods and disregards that the United States have sold goods worth 130 billion US dollar to China in 2017, is very telling about how trade relations with China are assessed by the US Government (United States Census Bureau 2019). China is not seen as a partner in a mutual beneficial trade relationship but as an enemy and the trade deficit is taken as proof that the United States are losing the "trade war with China". Consequently, US policy is only focused on shrinking the deficit, even though there is the real chance that this might hurt the US economy more than it helps.

The Trump government has suggested that it could reduce trade deficits simply by cutting imports However, imports enable US costumers to buy many products for a cheaper price than available from domestic production. Trade policies that aim at reducing US imports would increase prices and decrease the variety of available products, thereby lowering the living standard (Lawrence 2018, 1–2).

The fetish for the trade balance in exchanged goods as ultimate indicator has made US policy makers blind for other aspects of economic interaction between the United States and China. This chapter has shown that the United States profits more and China profits less from business ties than traditional trade statistics suggest. The foreign content share of products that the United States imports from China is around 32,2% which means that the value-added in China is remarkably reduced. Consequently, the 505 billion US dollar of goods that the United States imported from China in 2017 cannot be considered as revenue for China in its entirety. And also a trade balance that accounts for value-added still overestimates how much China profits from goods that cross the Pacific because a large share of these goods are produced by foreign firms mostly from Taiwan, Japan and Korea who shifted production facilities to China. The sales of these foreign companies to the United States are included in the Sino-American trade balance but only a share of the revenue stays in China.

At the same time the United States gets more returns than just what is exported directly from the United States to China. Some of the US companies with the highest revenue exposure to China produce lots of goods in third countries outside the United States and sell directly from abroad to China. US companies with subsidiaries and production sides in China are another source of income for the United States economy. An increasing amount of companies make more revenue with operations in China than with exports.

When all of these economic dimensions are considered economic interaction between China and the United States is much more balanced. Analysts of Deutsche Bank even estimated the United States had a 20 billion US dollar surplus in 2017 if sales of US companies with subsidies in China are included and exports of international companies from China to the United States are excluded from the calculation (Zhang and Xiong 2018).

Thus, from an economic perspective it is counterproductive for the United States to take measures against an important economic partner in order to reduce a supposed deficit and even to invoke a trade conflict based on the argument that the United States is already on the losing side and can only win by confronting China. In reality the trade balance in goods is not very meaningful for complex economic relations. This chapter has factored in additional dimensions of economic interaction to a come up with a more realistic estimation of how balanced economic relations between China and the United States are. Based on this assessment, it stands to reason that both sides benefit roughly equally from economic interaction. Furthermore, as has been illustrated in the previous chapters, the United States is highly dependent from exports to China and imports from China and has much to lose from a trade conflict.

4.4 China

4.4.1 Exports

The United States is China's most important export market with a total value of exported goods of 385,7 billion US dollar in 2016. Exports to the US made up 18,4% of China's global export volume which amounted to 2097,6 billion US dollar in 2016. That almost one fifth of a country's exports are shipped to a single trading partner is a rare constellation and shows how important the United States is as a sales market for Chinese products (UN Comtrade 2018).

Table 29: China - Top 10 Export Markets for Goods in 2016

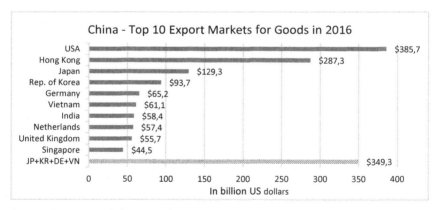

Source: (UN Comtrade 2018)

The next largest export market for China is the Special Administrative Region Hong Kong which is listed separately from Mainland China in UN trade statistics. Goods worth 287,3 billion US dollar passed the border from China to Hong Kong in 2016 which equals 13,7% of all Chinese exports in that year. This is a remarkably high export volume in relationship to the small size of Hong Kong. A population of only around 7 million people cannot consume that many goods. The explanation for the high exports to Hong

Kong is that China does not declare exports by final destination but only reports where goods were taken after they left China. However, the majority of goods that go from China to Hong Kong do not stay in Hong Kong but are shipped via Hong Kong's huge freight port to other countries (Feenstra and Hanson 2004, 3–4). Hong Kong is a global centre for intermediate trade and not only China is using Hong Kong as a trade hub. Goods that have initially been exported to Hong Kong and subsequently been re-exported to another country made up 491 billion US dollar of Hong Kong's global exports of 515 billion US Dollar. This means that around 95% of Hong Kong's exports are in fact re-exports (UN Comtrade 2018).

According to the Trade and Industry Department of the Hong Kong Government 58,1% of the 491 billion US dollar that Hong Kong re-exported in 2016 originated from Mainland China which are 285,3 billion US dollar (Hong Kong Trade and Industry Department 2017). This is very close to the 287,3 billion US dollar of total goods that Mainland China exported to Hong Kong in the same year which means that only goods worth 2 billion US dollar remained in Hong Kong. Therefore, Hong Kong is not an important sales market for Mainland China. It still has economic relevance for the Mainland as trade hub, but it is not relevant for an analysis of major export markets.

It is worth noting that 8,5% of Hong Kong's re-exports are sent to the United States which means that a large number of Chinese exports to Hong Kong are in fact exports to the United States. This explains a part of the statistical difference between the reported value of China's exports to the United States (385,7 billion US dollar) and the reported value of US imports from China (481,5 billion US dollar).

Since Hong Kong can be disregarded as export destination, the second largest destination for Chinese exports is Japan with an export volume of 129,3 billion US dollar. This is just one third of Chinese exports to the United States. The huge discrepancy in export volume between the two most important destinations for Chinese exports illustrates the unique significance of the United States as main costumer for Chinese products. Even combined exports to major trading partners Japan, South Korea, Germany, and Vietnam still only amount to 349,3 billion US dollar which is 36,4 billion US dollar less than exports to the United States. Having such a large customer who buys 18,4% of China's exports results in high sensitivity interdependence and not having adequate alternative export markets creates vulnerabilities since a loss of sales to the United States cannot sufficiently be compensated. Already this simple analysis of destinations for Chinese exports reveals an enormous economic dependence towards the United States.

The development of Chinese exports to the United States over time shows that exports have been on a low level for a long time and only started to grow exponentially in the early 2000s. Between the year 2000 and 2005 the export volume tripled from 52,1 billion US dollar to 163,1 billion dollar and within the next ten years it grew on average almost 10% each year to an all-time high of 409,9 billion US dollar in 2015. It only experienced a downturn during the height of the global financial crisis in 2009, which saw a global recession of exports, and more recently in the year 2016 when exports fell to 385,7 billion US Dollar (UN Comtrade 2018). Whether the latest decline of exports to the United States marks a reversal of the growth trend or is only a temporary event remains to be seen.

Table 30: China - Exports in Goods to USA since 1992

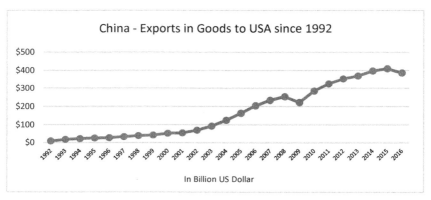

Source:(UN Comtrade 2018)

While the export volume was relatively small in the 1990s this does not mean the United States have not been an important export market during that time. A comparison between exports to the United States over time and exports to the world over time shows that the growth pattern is very similar. China's global export volume also only started to surge in the 2000s and had been on a low level before. Measured against a global export volume of 84,9 billion US dollar in 1992, exports to the US, which had a volume of 8,6 billion in 1992, made up 10,1% of all Chinese exports in that year. Until the year 2000 the share of exports to the United States in global Chinese exports had risen to 20,9% which is higher than it is today. Over the last five years exports to the USA constantly made up between 17% and 18,5% of all Chinese exports. This signifies two things. The dependence on the United States as main export market is not a new phenomenon and it is relatively stable on a high level in recent years. As dependence has consolidated over a long duration and is now well established, the United States has become a fundamental pillar for the Chinese export industry. Therefore, it is not easily possible to change and diversify the export strategy in order to become less dependent.

Table 31: China - Exports in Goods to World since 1992

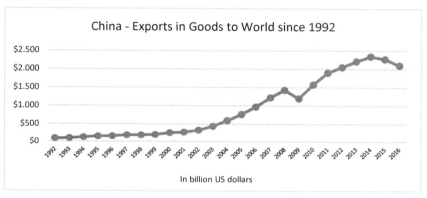

Source: (UN Comtrade 2018)

The observation that the growth of exports to the USA developed very similar to Chinese exports to the whole world is also significant for another reason. It illustrates that the rise of exports to the United States is not the result of a Chinese trade strategy that targets the United States but developed alongside a global expansion of Chinese trade ties which made China the world export champion. Today, the whole world receives huge amount of goods from China and not just the United States. The cause for the Chinese trade boom is the Chinese government's decision to move from economic self-sufficiency to an export-oriented development strategy. This policy started to pay off after the introduction of the so called "outward-oriented development strategy in the coastal areas" in 1988 (D. L. Yang 1991, 42). Driven by economic reforms and freer market access, GDP growth began to accelerate in the following years. (Yao 2011). As illustrated in table 32 exports became an increasingly important factor for the Chinese GDP. In 1989 exports had a share in GDP of 11%. The export-to-GDP-ratio grew slowly but steadily over the next decade and exceeded 20% in the year 2000. Between the year 2000 and 2006 the contribution of exports to China's economic success became very significant as the share of exports in GDP grew to more than 35%. In the following years, the ratio of exports to GDP descended back towards 20% and reached 19,7% in 2016.

It must be highlighted that the export-to-GDP-ratio is criticised for overestimating the impact of exports on economic growth because Chinese exports have a high share of foreign content. However, several studies have shown that exports are still very decisive for China's economic growth even when the value of foreign content is subtracted from Chinese exports. According to Akyüz the share of exports in GDP measured in value-added terms was about 20% in 2011. This is around 5% less than the share of gross exports in GDP for the same year (Akyüz 2011, 3). For the timeframe from 2002 to 2008 Yao calculated an average share of value-added exports in GDP of 15%, which is about 10% lower (Yao 2011). Much closer to the share of gross exports in GDP is the calculation by Zhu and Kotz who report value-added exports in GDP at 31,7% for 2007 compared to gross exports in GDP at 35,4% (A. Zhu and Kotz 2011). The deviation between these studies is quite strong and while they all show lower shares in GDP, the results are all above a 15% export-to-GDP ratio, which is still a significant contribution to the Chinese economy. As no complete value-added data set is available for the whole timeframe, share of exports in GDP will be used as a proxy, while noticing that the impact of exports is somewhat lower than this indicator suggests.

Table 32: China - GDP and Exports as Percentage of GDP since 1989

Source: (The World Bank 2018b)

The Chinese GDP started to grow faster at the same time when the share of exports in GDP began to pick up pace, but also continued to rise when the share of exports in GDP dropped back. Exports accelerated economic growth in China and with a share in GDP of 20% are still an important factor for China's economic success. However, it is also apparent that the impact of other factors on GDP growth have increased since 2006. These other factors are foremost domestic consumption and government spending. During the annual Central Economic Work Conference at the end of 2004 the Chinese government under former President Hu Jintao declared the intention to adjust the Chinese economic growth strategy from a heavily export- and invest-ment-driven approach towards a more consumption-driven economic development (Lardy 2006, 1).

The reason for this decision was to reduce the dependence on exports. China's Central Bank was afraid that an "increasing reliance on foreign trade […] will intensify external factor constraints" (The People's Bank of China 2005, 32–33). Naturally, an export-focused economy like China is vulnerable to fluctuations in the world economy. An economic crisis in another part of the world can have very negative ripple effects for a country whose GDP depends heavily on sales to foreign markets. Even when the economy of the exporting country is not directly affected by the crisis, it will suffer economic losses because trading partners who are directly affected will import less. Another so called "external factor restraint" is dependence on main trading partners and the leverage they get when foreign trade is decisive for the economic development of the exporting country. Cutting imports from China can be a weapon if the trade volume is relevant enough to have negative effects on Chinese economic growth. Therefore, stimulating domestic consumption was a logical step to make the Chinese economy less vulnerable. At the same time, it is also an indirect acknowledgement of a dependency towards the world market in general and towards its main trading partner, the United States, in particular.

As part of the shift in the growth strategy China adopted several policies to boost private spending. Taxes have been reduced, the minimum wage was increased, new subsidies have been introduced and spending for social programmes in the countryside was increased (Lardy 2006, 1–11). Initially these policies had little effect, but in combination with a positive demographic development and a general change in consumption behaviour, the share of consumer spending in GDP started to increase and helped the Chinese economy to keep up high economic growth rates. However, projections suggest that the share of consumption in GDP will not further rise in the next years. While consumption has become an important factor for economic growth, China has not been transformed to a truly consumption-driven economy and unless the Chinese government introduces extensive policy changes and drastically increases spending on health care, welfare, pensions and education, the prospects to further increase the share of consumption in GDP are low (Nie and Palmer 2016).

Since consumer spending is stagnating, at least for the time being, it is unlikely that the Chinese government can further reduce the dependency on exports. Without adequate compensation from the domestic market, China at least needs to keep up current export volumes in order to sustain the high economic growth rates it enjoyed over the last decades. It is no option for the communist leadership to accept low growth rates as part of their legitimacy is based on economic success.

---

3   According to Nie and Palmer younger generations in China consumer more (Nie and Palmer 2016, 28).

Unlike a democracy whose legitimacy is primarily based on elections, the Chinese Communist Party's legitimacy is based to a large degree on performance, which means that its rule is justified by the "accomplishment of concrete goals such as economic growth, social stability, and national unity" (Y. Zhu 2011, 124). Other sources of justification for one-party rule can be ideological legitimacy (value system), historical/traditional legitimacy (long rule), and charismatic legitimacy (respected leaders). All of these sources also contribute to the legitimacy of the Chinese Communist Party but communism as source of ideological legitimacy has declined along China's modernization towards a "capitalism with socialist characteristics", historical/traditional legitimacy is vague as history is always open to interpretation[4] and charismatic legitimacy depends on who is in power and how he is perceived, which means it varies heavily over time (H. Yang and Zhao 2015, 70–71). As other sources of legitimacy for the Chinese Communist Party are somewhat unreliable, performance legitimacy has become vital for its uncontested rule. The linkage between economic performance and support by the people is also reflected in survey data which show that Chinese who are pleased with economic conditions think more highly of the political system while those who rate economic conditions low also more often put one-party rule into questions (Chu 2013, 23).

Therefore, it is very important for the Chinese Communist Party to satisfy the people by improving economic conditions and by raising the standard of living. Since prosperity for all can only be achieved via economic growth, the Chinese Communist Party makes great efforts to sustain high growth rates (Y. Zhu 2011, 126). This had become evident during the 2008 global financial crisis, which was triggered by the subprime mortgage crisis in the United States. Ripple effects also hit China and resulted in a slowdown of economic growth. During the height of the crisis former Prime Minister Wen Jiabao said in a speech at the 2009 World Economic Forum:

"The international financial crisis has inflicted far-reaching impact on the world economy, and China's economy has not been immune. Our policies should [...] seek to bring a fundamental solution to the institutional and structural problems constraining the sound growth of China's economy [...] and raise the overall quality of economic and social progress." (Chinese Central Government 2009)

The Chinese government has been successful at keeping growth rates at high levels over decades, even despite major challenges like the global financial crisis. Thanks to the rapid economic development the quality of living in-

---

4 Traditionally, political legitimacy in the Chinese Empire was based on the "Mandate of Heaven" but when the last emperor was unable to modernise the country and could not ward off foreign aggressors this system was overthrown by the Kuomintang who in turn were overthrown by the Communist Party of China. The continued existence of the Kuomintang in Taiwan poses a serious challenges towards the historical legitimacy of the Communist Party of China.

creased tremendously and millions of Chinese escaped poverty and moved up to the middle class. Therefore, the Chinese Communist Party enjoys high support among the population and the legitimacy of the political system is not seriously questioned (H. Yang and Zhao 2015, 69). However, performance legitimacy brings with it that people grow accustomed to economic and social progress, which in turn raises expectations. People whose standard of living improved from year to year expect that this trend continues and become easily frustrated if living conditions stagnate or just slowly continue to improve (Blackwill and Campbell 2016, 13). Consequently, the Chinese government is always measured against past performances and compelled to constantly replicate successes. Even though the Chinese economy is well developed and the GDP growth rate is still way above world average with 6,7% in 2016, the Chinese leadership cannot rest on its laurels but is under constant pressure to sustain high growth rates (H. Yang and Zhao 2015, 69). This is all the more true as inequality widens in China which means that less wealthy people benefit less from GDP growth. Nowadays, increases in prosperity are for the most part distributed among the more affluent Chinese. Hence, GDP growth has to be high enough so that still plenty trickles down (Blackwill and Campbell 2016, 13).

Table 33: China - Annual GDP growth in Percentage

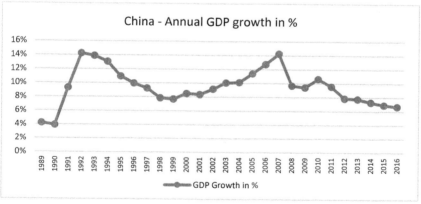

Source: (The World Bank 2018a)

China enjoyed very high growth rates throughout the last 25 years, but since 2007 growth is steadily slowing down and has fallen below 8% in recent years. Within the Chinese leadership 8% GDP growth per year was long seen as the lower limit to ensure broad public satisfaction and high social stability, but the Chinese government showed that they can still get along with slightly less than 7%. However, growth rates have left the "comfort zone" of the

Chinese Communist Party and President Xi Jinping's recent move towards stronger nationalism can be understood as a precaution, because appealing to nationalist sentiments is an alternative way to strengthen public support (Blackwill and Campbell 2016, 12).[5] It is impossible to say at which threshold slowing GDP growth will become a threat, but the Communist Party is getting worried in face of the negative growth trend.

From the data it is apparent that it becomes increasingly difficult for the Chinese government even to sustain the growth rate of the previous year. As mentioned above, the Chinese government introduced several spending programmes to stimulate domestic consumption and with that somewhat stabilised the slowing GDP growth in recent years. A side effect of governmental economic promotion in the form of tax incentives and subsidies is that the people become more dependent on the government. Once introduced, it is difficult to dismantle a spending programmes as this could stall the economy and hurts those people the most the spending was supposed to help. Therefore, the Chinese government is compelled to continue public spending (H. Yang and Zhao 2015, 80–81).

However, backing the Chinese economy with public spending cannot go on forever. China accumulated large reserves but increasing government expenditure resulted in budget deficits and dwindling savings. Furthermore, the effectiveness of spending programmes is reaching a limit. Public infrastructure projects do not give as high returns in GDP growth as before. The Chinese government spends more money every year but GDP growth is still slowing down (H. Yang and Zhao 2015, 82).

In this situation of slowing economic development China depends on exports as source of GDP more than ever. Rising public and consumer spending diversified the composition of the Chinese GDP but in order to sustain high growth rates also the export output must continue to grow. The United States has been a key market for the expansion of Chinese exports and due to the size of the population and its high purchasing power still offers vast potential to increase the volume of sales. Therefore, China is dependent on market access to the United States. Any restrictions on trade with its main export market would have negative effects on growth rates and in the long run could become a threat to the performance legitimacy of the Chinese Communist Party. History has shown that the Chinese population responds very sensitively to economic woes. Public unrests in 1986 and protests on Tiananmen

---

5   Xi Jinping is well advised not to push too hard on this issue because playing the nationalism card in order to create a rally around the flag effect can have very negative repercussions for China's foreign affairs. In a climate of resentment towards foreign countries, the leeway for international negotiations is severely limited. This was evident during an uprising of the territorial conflict between China and Japan regarding sovereignty over the Senkaku/Diaoyu islands. Anti-Japanese propaganda by Chinese state media resulted in public protests and looting of Japanese shops. This climate of resentment aggravated tensions and made it difficult for both governments to come to terms.

Square in 1989 have in part been motivated by economic factors (Blackwill and Campbell 2016, 12). Thus, the Chinese government is well advised to maintain good economic relations with the United States.

China's dependence on exports supports Cobden's argument, that the wealth and prosperity of a nation increasingly depends on economic interaction with other nations (Cobden 1903, 36); see page 17.

Exports by Product Category

The sheer size of Chinese exports to the United States already results in substantial dependence as 18,4% of all exports go the United States. But in some sectors of the Chinese economy even higher shares of world exports are sold to the United States. When exports to the United States are broken down into product categories and ranked by value it becomes obvious that the dependence on the US market is above average in the top six product categories; see table 34. Electrical equipment and electrical machinery (HS 85) has the highest value of all product categories with 93,2 billion US dollar of exported goods. 23,1% of China's global exports in this product category go to the United States which means that almost one in four electrical devises from China are sold in the United States. Machinery (HS 84) is the second most important product category in terms of value with an export volume of 79,5 billion US dollar and every fifth (19,9 %) mechanical appliance, engine or boiler exported by China is shipped to the United States (UN Comtrade 2018). The dependence on the US market is even higher for the categories furniture, bedding, mattresses (HS 94) and toys, games, sport requisites (HS 95). About one third of all exports in product categories HS 94 and HS 95 go the United States.

The ranking of product categories by value also signifies that heavy industries are not a major contributor to Chinese exports anymore. Among the top Chinese exports to the United States in 2016 are no product categories linked to steel or aluminium which used to be top seller goods. In 2008 China became the largest exporter of steel in the world but since then heavy industry was dismantled. Combined exports of product categories HS 72 (iron or steel) and HS 73 (iron and steel articles) to the United States in 2016 only amount to 9,5 billion US dollars. Steel and articles thereof are only the 11st most important export to the United States in terms of value and only 9,9% of China's worldwide steel exports go to the United States. This is way lower than the average of 18,4% that China exports to the United States across product categories. Chinese exports of aluminium and articles thereof (HS 76) to the United States even make up only 6,8% of global Chinese exports in that product category. Aluminium products worth 3,1 US dollars have been exported from China to the United States in 2016, which equals only rank 21 of all export product categories. All iron and aluminium exports to the United

States together only amount to 12,6 billion US dollars and thus are even less important for the Chinese export economy than exports of everyday products like toys and games (HS95) with an export volume of 14,8 billion US dollars or clothing, both knitted and not knitted (HS 61 and HS 62)[6], with a combined export volume of 30,4 billion US dollars (UN Comtrade 2018). Thus, it is fair to say that China's heavy industry is not a business sectors which relies heavily on the US market.

Table 34: China - Exports to USA by value of product category (HS2) and by percentage of world exports in 2016

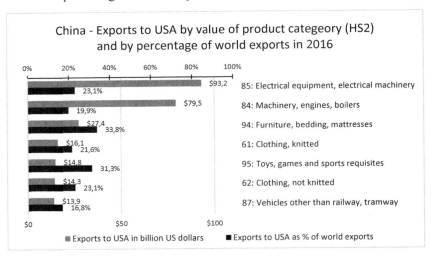

Source: (UN Comtrade 2018)[7]

As can be seen from table 34, there is a clear pattern that export categories with the highest value also depend the most on sales to the US market because a higher percentage of total exports, exceeding 19% for the top six categories, goes to the United States. Therefore, the United States is able to severely hurt the Chinese economy by restricting imports for only a few

6   Clothing is divided in product categories knitted clothing (HS 61) with an export volume of 16,1 billion US dollars and not knitted clothing (HS 62) with an export volume of 14,3 billion US.

7   The table "China - Exports to USA by value of product category" has different values than "USA – Imports from China by value of product category" due to trade data asymmetries which have been discussed in chapter 4.1. On average the value of product categories is lower in China's export statistics than in the United States' import statistics since Chinese exports to third countries (e.g. Hong Kong), which are re-exported United States, are classified as Chinese imports by US authorities.

product categories since this would shrink Chinese sales numbers significantly - though at a high price. As discussed in chapter 4.3.1. on US imports from China, the United States would not be able to sufficiently substitute Chinese imports in the product categories listed in table 34 and because HS 85 and HS 84 include numerous goods with high relevance to the US economy (e.g. computers, communication technology, semi-conductors, integrated circuits) this means that substantial costs would be associated with import restrictions. However, the sheer fact that the United States has the possibility to hurt China in this way means that the hold-up is bilateral. The buyer holds up the seller because there are not sufficient alternative buyers and the seller holds up the buyer because there are also not enough alternative sellers.

Computers

Chinese computer manufacturers are especially depended on sales to the United States. Computers (HS 8471) are the most important item in product category HS 84 because China exported desktop computers, servers, laptops, and tablet computers with a value of 39 billion US dollars to the United States in 2016. China's global computer sales amounted to 125 billion US dollars, which means that 31,2% or almost one in three computers from China are shipped to the United States (UN Comtrade 2018).

The most renowned Chinese computer manufacturer is Lenovo. Lenovo took over IBM's personal computer division in 2005, which was famous for the ThinkPad laptop. The acquisition raised Lenovo's global popularity and opened up new markets because it allowed to sell Lenovo laptops under the brand name ThinkPad. Mainly thanks to the strong sales of laptops Lenovo became the second largest retailer of computers in 2017 with a global market share of around 20%. The total revenue in 2017 amounted to 43 billion US dollars of which 13 billion US dollars (30%) came from sales on the American continent. Country specific data for the United States is not made public by Lenovo but it can be assumed that revenue from the United States makes up the majority of the 13 billion US dollars (Lenovo 2018). The Daiwa Security Group, a Japanese investment bank, estimates that between 20% and 25% of Lenovo's global revenue comes from the United States (Daiwa Security Group 2016). That would be a very substantial dependence on US market access.

However, Lenovo is not even the most dependent Chinese computer manufacturer. Even more dependent on US business are the little-known Chinese Original Design Manufacturer (ODM) and Original Equipment Manufacturer (OEM), who either design and produce personal computers which are subsequently rebranded and sold by international information technology companies or who just assemble computers according to the designs of foreign companies. The three largest suppliers of computers to the

United States are the Chinese subsidiaries of the Taiwanese ODMs/OEMs Quanta, Wistron and Compal. Their biggest customers are the US companies Apple, Dell, HP, Microsoft and Vizio.

Table 35: Top Suppliers of Computers (HS8471) to the United States

Company	Production Location	Main Costumers
Tech-Front (Quanta)	Chongqing, CN	Apple, Dell, HP, Vizio
Wistron Infocomm	Chengdu & Zhongshan, CN	Apple, Dell, HP, Microsoft
Compal Electronics	Kunshan, CN	Apple, Dell, HP

Source: (Descartes Datamyne 2018)

Tech-Front, a subsidiary of the Taiwan-based company Quanta, is located in the Chinese city Chongqing and produces the macbook air , the macbook pro and the apple watch for Apple (Apple 2018b, 20). Tech-Front also supplies Dell with the laptop product lines chromebook, inspiron and vostro (Dell 2017, 4). Other costumers of Tech-Front laptops include Hewlett-Packard and Vizio (Hewlett Packard 2017).

Wistron runs Chinese subsidiaries with factories in the cities Chengdu and Zhongshan, where a very large part of Dell's computer product line is manufactured including the chromebook laptop, the inspiron desktop computer, the inspiron laptop, the latitude laptop, the optiplex desktop computer, the venue tablet, the wyse desktop computer and the vostro laptop (Dell 2017, 4). Wistron also produces a large number of Hewlett-Packard laptops and desktop computers (Hewlett Packard 2017, 2). Smaller costumers include Apple, Motorola and Microsoft (Apple 2018b, 29).

Compal's main production side it located outside of Shanghai in Kunshan. They offer a broad range of ODM laptops, desktop computer, tablets, servers, smart home devises, televisions, computer monitors and even smart phones. Appel hired Compal as additional original equipment manufacturer for the apple watch (Apple 2018b, 5–6). Dell and Hewlett-Packard commissioned Compal as manufacturer for their popular laptop product lines (Hewlett Packard 2017, 1). In addition to the middle-class laptops inspiron, latitude and vostro, Compal also supplies Dell with the high-end laptops XPS and alienware (Dell 2017, 1). Compal states that 41,6% of its products are sold to companies on the American continent and because all main American costumers are located in the United States it can be concluded that practically all of the sales to the Americas go to the United States (Compal Electronics 2018).

The high dependence on US costumers is no surprise because US based information technology companies dominate the computer retailer market. In 2017 Hewlett-Packard, Dell and Apple had a combined market share for laptop computers of 49,1%, which means that basically every second laptop in the world was sold by one of these three US companies. They are also the biggest costumers of commissioned original design and original equipment computers, because they basically outsource all production to ODM or OEM companies, whereas Lenovo still operates its own factories and only out-sources small parts of its product line to contract manufacturers (Lenovo 2018, 259).

Table 36: Global Market Share for Laptop Computers in 2017

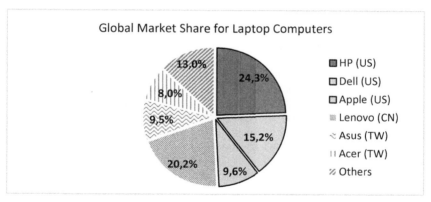

(TrendForce 2018)

The whole business model of Quanta, Wistron and Compal and other ODMs/OEMs is based on the business relationship with Hewlett-Packard, Dell and Apple. Without orders from the United States the huge Chinese production centres for ODM and OEM computers would be uneconomically and thousands of Chinese jobs would be endangered. The factory of Wis-tron's Chinese subsidiary in Zhongshan has 18.000 employees (Bieler and Lee 2017, 89), Tech-Front employs 70.000 workers in Chongqing (Quanta Computer 2018) and the factory of Compal's subsidiary in Kunshan had already 31.000 employees in 2013 (Compal Electronics 2013). It is estimated that in total around 411.000 Chinese workers are employed in the computer manufacturing industry (Bieler and Lee 2017, 285–97). Furthermore, Chinese companies in the computer manufacturing supply chain who produce computer hardware parts would also be affected.

Once more it must be noted that the hold-up is bilateral. Computer retailer who have no own production are just as depended on original design and original equipment manufacturer as ODMs/OEMs without direct distribution are dependent on retailers. The relationship is almost symbiotic because the business success of the ODMs/OEMs is tied to the sales numbers of the computer retailers. At the same time, the retailer's success also relies on the quality and the reliability of the supplier. Any disturbance of the business relationship due to political disagreements or restrictions to free trade will have negative consequences for US retailers as well as for Chinese suppliers.

Dependence on Exports

China's export to the United States have expanded drastically and over the last two decades. While this development coincided with a general expansion of Chinese exports, the United States still stand out because they are by far the most important export destination for Chinese goods with exports adding up to 385,7 billion US dollars in 2016. Exports to the second most important export partner Japan, setting aside Hong Kong due to the large share of re-exports, only amounted to 129,3 billion US dollars in 2016 which is just about one-third of exports to the United States.

Compared to China's total export volume, exports to the United States constantly made up between 17% and 18,5% over the last five years. For many Chinese export-oriented companies the United States is the most important sales market and several industry sectors, as for instance computer manufacturing, have adjusted production according to the needs of US costumers. The Chinese focus on the US market resulted in a deep-rooted dependence on exports to the United States that cannot be dissolved without suffering significant economic losses because diversifying production and finding new export markets or expanding existing markets takes time and requires new investments. Even in the long run it is very unlikely that China will be able to fully compensate exports to the USA because the United States is the largest consumer market in the world according to household final consumption expenditure. US citizens have a high available income and are keen to consume which makes the United States basically an indispensable trading partner for any export-oriented country (The World Bank 2016).

That China cannot give up on the sales opportunities of the US market ties China to the United States and gives the US leverage. Even more so since China's GDP depends heavily on exports. The communist party tries hard to reduce China's export dependency and was quite successful in stimulating domestic consumption, but it was not enough to change the orientation of the economy. China remains an export-oriented economy and the export industry continues to be the main pillar of Chinese economic development.

As a main destination of Chinese exports, the United States would be able to exert pressure on GDP growth figures by restricting Chinese exports. The possibility to negatively influence China's GDP is a tool of power because the legitimacy of the communist party is based to a large part on performance; and not on democratic elections. Economic performance is the safest way to satisfy people and to secure support for the political system. Thus, maintaining good trade relationships with the United States and securing market access for Chinese goods is in the communist party's own interest.

US market access is especially decisive for Chinese producers of communication technology, computers, semi-conductors, and integrated circuits. The information and communication technology industry sector is particularly export-oriented and the US is the main export destination. This industry sector also has the biggest share in Chinese exports to the US since the two product groups HS 85 and HS 84, to which most goods of this industry sector belong, make up 44,7% of all Chinese exports to the United States; 172,5 billion US dollars out of 385,7 billion US dollars (UN Comtrade 2018).

Using the computer manufacturing industry, which belongs to product group HS 84, as examples, it was demonstrated in detail how much certain industry sectors depend on economic cooperation with the US. Chinese computer manufacturer like Lenovo, who directly sell computers to end-costumers, depend on the US market because US costumers buy a great number of computers. Lenovo assumedly earns between 20% to 25% of its global revenue with sales to the US. Original design manufacturer (ODMs) and original equipment manufacturer (OEMs), who do not sell to end-costumers, depend on American computer retailers because they are the most important costumers of ODM/OEM computers. While the largest ODMs/OEMs computer manufacturer are Taiwan-based, they produce almost exclusively in China and contribute extraordinarily to the Chinese economy. Compal, one of the top ODM/OEM, states that more than 40% of its revenue comes from commissioned work for US tech companies like Dell, HP, Apple (Compal Electronics, 2018).

Orders from US companies ensure high capacity utilization in all companies that produce computers and other information technology. Whole regions have specialised on the production of components and final assemblage. The Pearl River Delta with the city of Guangdong as major hub has been the first region that attracted ODM/OEM companies because the proximity to Hong Kong facilitates exports. Another centre of the IT industry is the Yangtze River Delta region which surrounds Shanghai. More recently the cities of Chengdu and Chongqing entered the business and have become hotspots for the assemblage of consumer electronics like smart phones or tablet computers (Bieler and Lee 2017, 285–97). The business model of these economic regions depends strongly on US exports. Millions of jobs would be at risk if trade between the US and China would be interrupted.

4.4.2 Imports

The US is the fourth most important import partner for China and the most important one outside of East Asia. According to UN trade statistics China imported goods with a value of 135,1 billion US dollars from the US in 2016. This equals roughly 8,5% of China's total imports from around the world. The only countries which have a higher share in China's global imports are Taiwan (8,7%), Japan (9,2%) and South Korea (10,0%), all of which are close neighbours bordering the East China Sea (UN Comtrade 2018).

Table 37: China - Top 10 Import Markets for Goods in 2016

China - Top 10 Import Markets for Goods in 2016

Country	Value
Rep. of Korea	$159,0
Japan	$145,7
Taiwan	$138,8
USA	$135,1
Germany	$86,1
Australia	$70,9
Malaysia	$49,3
Brazil	$45,9
Switzerland	$39,9
Thailand	$38,5

In billion US dollars

Source: (UN Comtrade 2018)

A large part of imports from South Korea, Japan and Taiwan are intermediate goods which are further processed in China. Many companies from these three countries offshored parts of their production chains to subsidiary companies in China or to Chinese partner firms. Typically, production steps at the end of the production chain are conducted in China. Sometimes this only involves assemblage, but more often also some parts are manufactured in China and combined with imported intermediate inputs (Xing 2014, 115). A large part of products with intermediate inputs from South Korea, Japan and Taiwan are not sold in China but shipped to third countries – mainly the US and Europe. A typical example for such a triangular trade pattern are laptop computers. The more advanced microchips like the ones used in graphics processing units are often still manufactured in South Korea, Japan and Taiwan. They are exported to China as intermediate parts and combined with other imported or domestically produced integrated-circuits and semiconductors to manufacture the finished laptop. Some of these laptops remain in China but the majority is made for export to large markets in America and

Europe (Lovely and Liang 2018, 3). This means that, in practice, imports from East Asian trade partners are often re-exported as part of processed goods.

Table 38: Processing imports as part of triangular trade

Source: (Van Assche 2012, 11)

China also imports intermediate goods from countries outside East Asia, but they make up a smaller part of total imports from those countries. Therefore, imports from other trading partners more often remain in China. It is important to differentiate between imports which are designated for the Chinese market and those who are imported only for the purpose of re-export, because items that remain in China have a higher value for the Chinese economy. These are goods for which Chinese people and companies have a high domestic demand. Either because they are not available in China at all or not in sufficient quantity or because China does not have the know-how to produce these goods domestically.

That is not to say that imports of intermediate goods are not important for the Chinese economy. The high amount of intermediate imports is the result of China's integration into international value chains which has contributed greatly to the economic development of the last decades. However, intermediate imports which are not consumed in China only have relevance for the specific value chain to which they belong and not to the whole Chinese economy. As already mentioned, Chinese companies are often located at the end of a value chain where the added value and the profit margin is lower than for foreign companies which are located upstream in the value chain.[8] Consequently, the proportion of value added for China in the triangular trade with processed goods is not very high which means that the relevance of intermediate imports for the Chinese economy is limited. A microchip that is imported by China only to be put into a laptop that is exported from China to the United States has not the same relevance for the Chinese economy as machines or engines which China imports for the construction of industrial facilities like e.g. power plants. Thus, in an assessment of the importance of import partners it must be taken into account how much of Chinese imports from a partner country are ultimately re-exported.

---

8   For this reason, tariffs on Chinese processing exports hurt the Chinese economy less than economies located upstream in the value chain i.e. South Korea, Japan and Taiwan.

The Chinese customs office provides data which allows concluding how much of Chinese imports are designated for export because they differentiate between so called processing imports and regular imports. Processing imports are defined as imports of goods solely for the purpose of further processing and re-export. If a company declares imports as processing imports, they are exempt from duties but cannot be sold on the Chinese market. From January to July 2018 a total of 21,1% of Chinese imports have been declared as processing imports (General Administration of Customs of the People's Republic of China 2018).

Table 39: Distribution of China's processing imports by country

Country	Share of total processing imports
Japan	20,4%
South Korea	17,3%
Taiwan	15,8%
United States	7,4%

Source: (Van Assche 2012, 11)

The Chinese customs office does not provide a breakdown of processing imports by country, but in a study from 2012 van Assche was able to calculate the distribution of China's total processing imports by country; see table 39. According to von Assche's calculation 20,4% of China's processing imports come from Japan, which makes Japan the most important source of intermediate goods. South Korea and Taiwan follow closely with 17,3% and 15,8% respectively. Taken together 53,5% of all Chinese processing imports come from just these three countries. The US is also a source of processing imports but with share of 7,4% of total Chinese processing imports it does not come close to the amounts of intermediate goods that China imports from neighbouring countries. While these numbers do not tell how much of Chinese imports are domestically consumed, they allow the conclusion that imports from the United States are much less frequently re-exported than imports from Japan, South Korea and Taiwan (Van Assche 2012, 11).

Determining where imports are finally consumed is complicated and just very few studies who do this calculation for Chinese imports differentiate by countries of origin. The most recent calculation is from 2012 but it only covers South Korea and Japan. Johnson and Noguera combined input-output tables and bilateral trade data to reveal all final and intermediate goods linkages between selected country pairs. Based on these linkages they constructed a synthetic table that describes where exports from South Korea and Japan to China are consumed (Johnson and Noguera 2012, 235).

Table 40: Imports from South Korea and Japan and destination of ultimate consumption

Imports from	Consumed in China	Consumed in third country
South Korea	61,3%	38,7%
Japan	64,5%	35,8%

Source: (Johnson and Noguera, 2012, p. 235)

According to Johnson and Noguera only 61,3% of goods from South Korea and 64,5% of goods from Japan remain in China and are consumed by the domestic economy. The other 38,7% and 35,8% respectively are either redirected to a third country or reflected to the country of origin (Johnson and Noguera 2012, 235). Thus, more than one third of the goods that China imports from South Korea and Japan are of lesser value for the Chinese economy as they are only imported for processing and re-export. Not having data for the location of consumption of imports from the US makes a direct comparison impossible but distribution of China's total processing imports by country shows that the US is a less important source for intermediate imports. Given these findings it is safe to say that the domestic consumption rate for imports from the US to China is higher than for South Korea and Japan. Imports from the US have a higher share of goods that China actually needs which raises the importance of the United States as import partner. If processing imports are disregarded, the US might even be the most important import partner by value of imports because this would reduce the value of imports from South Korea and Japan by more than one third, while the value of imports from the US would not drop by the same amount. Once more it is evident that looking at raw data can be misleading as not only the quantity but also the quality of traded goods defines how important trade relations are.

Imports by Product Category

To determine what the goods are that China needs from the United States, more information about the quality and composition of Chinese imports from the United States is required. Table 41 lists the product categories with the highest import value. Import value is a good indicator for the importance of imported goods because it shows how high the Chinese demand is. In addition, the table also displays imports from the US as percentage of China's global imports for each of the product categories. The higher the proportion of US imports, the more difficult it is for China to find alternative suppliers. Consequently, the share in world imports can be used as indicator for Chinese sensitivity dependence across product categories.

The product categories with the highest value among all imports are electrical equipment and electrical machinery (HS 85) with 15,8 billion US dollars and machinery, engines and boilers (HS84) with 14,5 billion US dollars. These two categories belong to Advanced Technology Products and together with the categories aircraft (HS 88) and optical, photographic, medical apparatus (HS 90) a total of four out of the six most important product categories are composed of Advanced Technology Products (UN Comtrade 2018).

Table 41: China - Imports from USA by value of product category (HS2) and by percentage of world imports in 2016

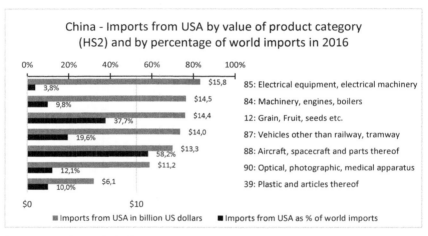

Source: (UN Comtrade 2018)

Advanced Technology Products are difficult to manufacture and require long-term investments into research and development (R&D), which is why emerging economies like China cannot easily substitute these goods with domestic production but are dependent on imports from countries with more advanced high-technology sectors.

Microchips

Microchips, which belong to HS 85, are a good example of an Advanced Technology Product that China still has to import on a large-scale. Even though the Chinese government invested heavily in a local industry for integrated circuits (HS 8542) and semi-conductors (HS 8541), Chinese companies still lack behind as their self-designed microchips are two to three generations behind the latest state of the art. Instead Chinese manufacturer produce mainly lower-end microchips for low margin consumer segments (SEMI

2017, 24–39). The global market share of Chinese-designed integrated circuits ranges from 0% up to 22% depending on the model type. Chinese manufacturers have a relatively high market share for communication processors, which for example power wireless LAN systems, but this technology is not that advanced anymore. Chinese microchips are also commonly used in smartphone cameras and fingerprint sensors, which do not require a very high processing power. However, China has zero percent market share in more advanced designs like embedded MPUs, which combine several types of integrated circuits in one module and are used for new technologies like cloud computing and internet of things. China also has no domestic production of micro processing units (MPU) but needs to import this central component of every server or personal computer (SEMI 2017, 24).

Table 42: China – Market Share for Integrated Circuit Designs

Market Share of Chinese Manufacturers for Integrated Circuit Designs			
System	Device	Integrated Circuit	Made in China
Processor/MCU	Server	MPU	0%
	PC	MPU	0%
	Industrial	MCU	2%
FPGA/DSP	Programable Logical	FPGA/EPLD	0%
	Digital Process	DSP	0%
Communication System	Mobile Communication	Application Processor	18%
		Comm. Processor	22%
		Embedded MPU	0%
		Embedded DSP	0%
	Core Network	NPU	15%
Storage Devices	Semicon Storage	DRAM	0%
		NAND Flash	0%
		Nor Flash	5%
Display & Video	HD TV & Smart TV	Image Processor	5%
		Display Driver	0%

Source: (SEMI 2017, 24)

But it is not only a question of quality but also of quantity. According to Semiconductor Equipment and Materials International (SEMI), an association of microchip manufacturers, China had a demand for integrated circuits (HS 8542) of 104 billion US dollars in 2015 but local production only amounted to 13,2 billion US dollars, which means that China can only satisfy 12,7% of its demand locally (SEMI 2017, 9).

That Chinese microchip manufacturers are unable to produce enough microchips to satisfy the domestic demand and lack the know-how for high-end microchips, makes the Chinese IT sector very dependent on imports and technology transfer. The Chinese government openly acknowledges that this dependency is a veritable vulnerability as this quote from China's minister of industry and information, Miao Wei, in the state-run newspaper China Daily documents:

"With overseas firms controlling most of the high-end microchip exports to China, we realized that it is important to develop our own microchips to avoid bottlenecks for the IT industry." (China Daily 2015)

Despite Beijing's awareness of the issue, China was so far not able to close the technological gap. The development cycle of microchips is rather short, but each advancement requires year's or even decades of research. As soon as Chinese companies successfully developed their own designs or reverse engineered the latest microchips, foreign companies have already developed the next generation or even the generation after the next. To speed up the chase for technological equality Chinese microchip companies tried to acquire know-how by taking over foreign companies, but so far foreign governments successfully blocked Chinese acquisitions (Quartz 2018c). The United States is especially cautious and even prevents acquisitions of US chip manufacturers by companies with large Chinese investors. The issue of technology transfer in the microchip sector has become a high priority in US politics or otherwise President Trump and President Obama before him would not have stepped in themselves in two cases. President Obama even prevented the sales of a German supplier for the semiconductor industry to Chinese investors on the grounds that the German company has a subsidiary in the United States. This exemplifies how badly the United States wants to prevent any technology transfer to China (China State Council 2018, 45).

Despite all efforts, some technology transfer takes place because several foreign companies formed joint-ventures with Chinese microchip developers (Quartz 2018c). According to the American Chamber of Commerce in China it is common practice that government officials pressurise American companies with joint-ventures in China to share intellectual property and technology (AmCham China 2017, 86). To what extent foreign companies yield to the pressure out of fear to lose market access is unclear because companies that admit technology transfer to China draw criticism from politicians in their home countries and thus many keep silent about it. Quartz, a portal for the tech industry, claims foreign companies mainly share know-how about established technologies with their Chinese joint-venture partners and largely resist to disclose top-notch technology (Quartz 2018c). There is much to be said for this assessment because sharing important company secrets means to give up a company's competitive advantage. This is a very high price to pay for access to the Chinese market, so it seems likely that foreign companies indeed do not share the latest technological innovations, but only that know-how which is required to outsource mass production to China.

From the above follows that China will not be able to catch up with leading microchip manufacturers anytime soon and continues to be dependent on imports of high-end microchips. This dependence is very relevant for trade relations between China and the United States because the US is not only the country where microchips were invited but continues to be the key supplier for high-end microchips. US companies lost market shares in the last decades but still almost one in two microchips are produced by the American microchip industry (Semiconductor Industry Association 2018). In addition, American companies completely dominate the market for microprocessors and graphic processing units (GPU). Intel and AMD have a duopoly on x86-based microprocessors which power basically all PCs and Laptops. AMD shares another duopoly on GPUs, commonly known as graphics cards, with the American competitor Nvidia. This market constellation enables the United States to cut off China from supplies of some of the most important products in the age of information technology (Quartz 2018b).

It must be noted that once more the mere trade numbers are not very telling and not point to a very high dependence on imports of US microchips. In 2016 China imported integrated circuits (HS 8542) worth 8,7 billion US dollars from the United States which is more than half of all imports from product category HS 85 and by far the single most important product sub-category by import value, but for China 8,7 billion US dollars is only about 3% of its global microchip imports. However, in this case the quantity is less important than the quality since what China is mainly importing from the US are high-end microchips and many of these are only available from US producers – e.g. x-86 based microprocessors and GPUs (UN Comtrade 2018).

In addition, actual Chinese imports of microchips from US companies are way higher than what is reported in trade statistics. As has been discussed in chapter 4.3.2.5, US microchip producers have outsourced large parts of production to foreign countries. According to the US Semiconductor Industry Association at least 50% of manufacturing plants are located outside the United States (Semiconductor Industry Association 2018). If a Chinese company imports Skyworks microchips from a plant in Mexico, Skyworks' largest one, they do not show up in trade statistics because they have not been shipped from the United States to China (Skyworks 2016, 123). Therefore, China in fact receives a much higher volume of microchips from US companies than just the reported 8,7 billion US dollars of imported integrated circuits (HS 8542).

Another factor that has to be considered are microchips produced under license. Several Chinese microchip manufacturers who lack the know-how for designing high-end microchips use blueprints and patents of US companies. License production safes time and money as no physical shipments are required and the US microchip developer can make extra profit without any further investments into production facilities and logistics. Not every US microchip company issues licenses and some are more careful than others about which microchip designs are release for licensed production, but those companies engaged in the licence business make most revenue with Chinese licensees. Qualcomm is the extreme example because licence fees and royalties from Chinese manufacturers make up as much as 18,85% of the company's global revenue (Qualcomm 2017, 16 & 29). Without licensed production China would need to import even more microchips including high-end designs. Thus, licensing is another source of dependence on the US microchip industry and has to be added to the total calculation.

Adding licensed production makes the United States still not China's largest source for microchips, but it is a way more important supplier than the import volume suggests and hard to replace. That said, what matters even more is that the United States is the most important supplier for high-end microchips. Chinese companies will not be able to substitute US high-end microchip imports with own designs for the years to come because they still lack far behind in research and technology transfer is limited through intervention by US politics. Due to the monopoly position of US microchip developers for certain chip designs China cannot fall back on alternative suppliers and will continue to depend on imports of US high-end microchips and access to US microchip designs via licensing agreements. Consequently, China is very vulnerable to any US restrictions on microchip supplies despite a relative moderate trade volume.

This vulnerability became apparent in April 2018 when the US Department of Commerce issued a ban on sales to the Chinese telecommunication systems provider ZTE. The company, which produces all kinds of telecommunication equipment including mobile phones and network routers, admitted to violations of US sanctions by exporting telecommunication devises to North Korea and setting up telecommunication networks in Iran. After an initial settlement agreement between ZTE and US authorities in 2017, the US Department of Commerce declared in April 2018 that ZTE had mislead the US government and failed to provide full disclosure. As a consequences a seven-year embargo against ZTE was put into effect. Due to this sanction ZTE was no longer able to acquire anything from the United States including processed goods which include US parts (U.S. Department of Commerce 2018).

This was a major issue because ZTE's most important microchip supplier is Qualcomm with whom it also has multiple license agreements for 3G and 4G products (Qualcomm 2015). The dependence on this single US company is tremendous as around 70% of ZTE'S mobile phones feature Qualcomm microchips. Overall, 80-90% of ZTE devises contain at least one US component or use US software (The Economist 2018). Since the company's supply chain depends so heavily on US hard- and software ZTE had to suspend production within a few weeks after the embargo took effect and was soon on the verge of bankruptcy (Quartz 2018a). This exemplifies how much leverage the US government has on the Chinese IT sector. The vulnerability dependence of Chinese high-tech companies like ZTE is so high that the United States can put them out of business.

However, it must also be considered that the embargo had negative consequences for US suppliers like Qualcomm who lost a major costumer. Putting ZTE out of business would have backfired on the US economy which is very likely the reason why the United States came to terms with ZTE after two months. The new settlement included among others a one billion US dollars penalty and monitoring by an US compliance team. That President Trump and President Xi were involved in the negotiations means both governments considered the issue to be significant for national interests (Quartz 2018a).

The ZTE settlement is a prime example of Montesquieu's definition of interdependence as a relationship in which one has an interest in buying and the other one has an interest in selling. As the needs are mutual, both parties are encouraged to find a solution so that cooperation can continue (Montesquieu as cited in Hirschman 1977, 80). While the United States is able to exploit Chinese dependence on US technology, it can only do so by hurting its own economy which leads to a lose-lose situation. So there is not only an incentive to continue trade cooperation in the microchip sector, but also to avoid confrontation because a discontinuation of trade would inflict losses on both sides. However, if the United States, for whatever reason, wishes to exploit the Chinese dependence on microchip imports and accepts to suffer the costs that are associated with an export ban, it can deal a heavy blow to the Chinese IT industry.

Aircraft

Another example of an Advanced Technology Product that China cannot so easily produce domestically and for which it depends on imports from the US are airplanes. Airplanes belong to product category HS 88 which includes all aircraft, spacecraft and parts thereof. With a total of 13,3 billion US dollars of imports in 2016 it is a product category with high demand from China. What makes this category stand out is that China bought 58,2% of all imported aircraft and spacecraft from the United States which means that China has a high sensitivity dependence on US imports from HS 88. The most important item within this product category are large commercial airplanes because out of the 13,3 billion US dollars imports from category HS 88 China spend 12,4 billion US dollar for products belonging to sub-chapter HS 880240, which is defined as aeroplanes of an unladen weight exceeding 15,000kg. In absolute numbers China imported 210 out of 361 airplanes exceeding 15,000kg from the United States. The only American aircraft manufacturer for airplanes of this category is Boeing which means that China imported almost 60% of large commercial airplanes from a single company.

At first glance this market constellation for HS 880240 might seem more unfavourable for the United States because China could in theory just buy large commercial airplanes from Boeing's competitors instead. In fact, it would be very easy for the Chinese government to enforce a boycott against Boeing as all airplane purchases are handled by the state-owned China Aviation Supplies Holding Co. who distributes airplanes to Chinese airlines. Since Boeing has a high dependence on the Chinese market - one in every four Boeing airplanes is exported to China - this would have far-reaching consequences for America's single most important aircraft company (Aero 2018). However, the dependence is reciprocal because there is only one other company in the world who manufactures large commercial airplanes and that is the European Airbus SE (CAPA 2018). The Canadian Bombardier Inc. offers some medium-size airplanes which belong to HS 880240, but they only have a regional operation range and a maximum capacity of 104 passengers (Bombardier 2017). Therefore, Bombardier is not a competitor for long-range or wide-body aircrafts with a high passenger capacity.

If a market is dominated by only two companies, this constellation is called duopoly. Different market mechanisms apply in a duopoly than in a constellation with high competition. If China would boycott Boeing it would have no more leverage in negotiations with Airbus. Airbus would gain a de-facto monopoly for the Chinese market which means that they could dictate prices. Without any competitor to turn to China would also have very limited options to react to delivery delays or quality defects. Not to mention that Airbus might not be capable of increasing production quickly enough to satisfy the high demand for new airplanes in China. Therefore, boycotting Boeing would be very painful and costly for the Chinese aviation sector.

From the US perspective the duopoly in the market for large commercial airplanes provides the opportunity to cause harm to the Chinese aviation sector by imposing an embargo on aircraft exports to China. But only at the cost of ruining business prospects for one of Americas strongest export industries. As no party is able to inflict costs on the opposing party without creating negative repercussions for themselves, the bilateral economic relationship in the aircraft and aviation sector is truly interdependent. A trade conflict between the United States and China would create a lose-lose situation because Boeing does not want to lose Chinese customers and Chinese Airlines do not want to be at the mercy of Airbus. Thus, the constellation in the aircraft sector is similar to the microchip sector and also generates a strong incentive for continued cooperation and a disincentive to engage in a trade conflict.

Besides microchips and aircraft, there is another product category among the six most important ones that contains Advanced Technology Products. China imported 11,2 billion US dollars of optical, photographic, and medical apparatus (HS 90) in 2016. Product category HS 90 includes high-tech goods like radar equipment, laser, geophysical and meteorological instruments, spectrometer, chromatographs, pacemaker, x-ray scanner or magnetic resonance imaging scanner. 12,1% of all global imports of these kinds of goods came from the United States, which constitutes a considerable sensitivity dependence (UN Comtrade 2018). The most important subgroup within product category HS 90 is medical devices. China imported medical devises with a value of 6,6 billion US dollars from the United States in 2016. Thus, medical devices account for more than half of the 11,2 billion US dollars of imports from HS 90. According to the China Chamber of Commerce for Import and Export of Medicines and Health Products 32,8% of all medical devices that China imported in 2016 are from the United States (CCCMHPIE 2017).

China has a very high demand for medical devices because the equipment in most healthcare facilities is low-standard and outdated. The Chinese medical technology industry is underdeveloped and lacks technological expertise. Approximately 80% of domestic medical device manufacturer only produce low-end equipment, e.g. catheters and tubing, or midrange devices like ultrasound scanner or electrocardiogram (ECG) machines (China Med Device 2018). Therefore, China depends on high-end medical device imports to improve the healthcare system and public health. The United States is the number one supplier of advanced medical diagnostic machines, state-of-the-art imaging equipment and high-precision surgical instruments. Two of the world's largest medical device manufacturer, GE Healthcare and Johnson & Johnson Medical Devices, are American companies and according to the US Department of Commerce there is a particularly high demand in China for medical devices of these companies (International Trade Administration 2017).

Table 43: China – Import of Medical Devices from Top 3 Countries

China's most important import markets for medical devices (% of total imports)		
Country	Volume of imports	% of Medical Device Imports
United States	6,6 billion US dollars	32,8%
Germany	3,4 billion US dollars	16,8%
Japan	2,4 billion US dollars	11,8%

Source: (International Trade Administration 2017).

Germany and Japan are the main competitors to the United States in the medical device market. In 2016 16,8% of China's medical device imports came from Germany and 11,8% from Japan. That China's second largest import market for medical devices provides only half the volume of the United States demonstrates how important the US is as supplier of medical technology. Even taken together Germany and Japan deliver less medical devices to China than the United States, but compared with the aircraft industry the market constellation is more diverse as China rather evenly sources one third of medical devices from the United States, one third from Germany and Japan and one third from the rest of the world (International Trade Administration 2017). The German medical technology company Siemens Healthineers is on par with American competitors in terms of size as well as know-how (ProClinical 2018) and Japan, while not having a global market leader in the medical technology sector, has a great number of medium size medical device manufacturer who are leading in specific subfield of the sector (McKinsey 2017). Thus, China has real alternatives for some of the healthcare technology it currently obtains from the United States. However, compensating 32,8% of medical device imports is challenging and takes time. If the United States would restrict exports of medical devises, China would suffer economic consequences during the adaptation phase and also the modernisation of the healthcare system would be impacted, but due to the more diverse market constellation replacing US supplies seems possible in the medium term.

In the long run China has even the chance to become more independent by expanding the domestic medical technology industry. Thanks to government assistance some Chinese medical device manufacturer have already become competitive in medium-level technologies niches. The US Department of Commerce expects the Chinese government to increase investments even more and assumes that Chinese companies will eventually be able to close the technological gap (International Trade Administration 2017). But for now, China still has a considerable vulnerability dependence in this economic sector which gives the United States additional leverage.

Agricultural Products

While Advanced Technology Products like microchips, aircraft and medical devices dominate Chinese imports from the United States, it is remarkable that the third most important import product category by value is grain, fruit and seeds (HS 12). China imported 14,4 billion US dollars in agricultural products from HS 12 in 2016, which is more than China spends on imports of aircrafts or medical devices from the United States. Since grain, fruit and seeds have a low unit price an incredibly high quantity of food is crossing the pacific. The United State is the second most important supplier as 37,7% of all imported grain, fruit and seeds (HS 12) come from the US and is only outranged by Brazil from which China purchases 40,6%. Together Brazil and the United States account for 78,3% of all grain, fruit and seed imports, which comes close to dual sourcing (UN Comtrade 2018).

Table 44: China - Imports of grain, fruits and seeds (HS 12) in 2016

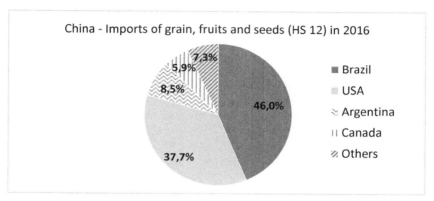

Source: (UN Comtrade 2018)

China's high dependence on two suppliers does not necessarily pose a problem for this product category because agricultural goods are easier to substitute as Advanced Technology Products. The food industry requires less know-how and it is easier for a government to build up a larger agricultural sector than to establish a modern high-tech sector. However, China has a population of about 1,4 billion people and thus requires vast amounts of food to ensure sufficient supply.

Over the last decades China was able to increase food production considerably and achieved a food self-sufficiency of 94,5% in 2015, but even in a country as big as China fertile soil and water are limited (Huang et al. 2017, 2941). Furthermore, huge cultivation areas have been lost due to industrial pollution. Approximately one-sixth of Chinese soil is contaminated with heavy metals or toxic chemicals (CSIS 2017). At the same time the population continues to grow and because of the increased prosperity people consume more food. Therefore, China had to increase food imports in recent years. An evaluation of several studies regarding China's future food security, which was published in the journal of the Chinese Academy of Agricultural Sciences, forecasts that food self-sufficiency will drop to 91% until 2025 (Huang et al. 2017, 2941). Especially worrisome is the supply of cereals like rice or wheat, potatoes, and soybeans. Self-sufficiency for these kinds of agricultural products dropped from 97% in 2001 to 86% in 2015 and is expected to drop even further in the future (Huang et al. 2017, 2934). This means China will need to import even more food than it currently does and thus will becomes more dependent on large food exporters like the United States. Chinese food security studies even raise the concern if enough food supply is available on the world market to satisfy the rising Chinese demand. For the year 2025 it is calculated that if global food production would remain on the same level as in 2015 Chinese demand would reach up to 80% of world exports for some foodstuff. As other fast-growing countries like India are also expected to import more food, shortages for a number of foodstuff like soybeans, oilseeds, maize or dairy would be the consequence. However, Chinese agricultural experts assume that global food production will continue to increase and for that reason they expect that China will be able to satisfy its demand for all foodstuff (Huang et al. 2017, 2940–42).

The problem with these kinds of food security projections is that they are based on the assumption that China will have unrestricted access to the global market. If China is only able to satisfy its rising demand for certain foodstuff if global production is increased, it raises the question how well China could compensate the loss of a major supplier. Some of the foodstuff for which limited global supply is expected, like soybeans (HS1201) or oilseeds (HS 1204), belongs to product category grain, fruit and seeds (HS 12). If the United States would restrict exports of product category HS12 China would need to find new suppliers for 37,7% of imported grain, fruit and seeds (UN Comtrade 2018). Given the projected scarce availability of soybeans and oilseeds, it stands to reason that China would not be able to import enough of these products to satisfy all demand.

This would have serious consequences for the meat and dairy industry in China because soybeans and oilseeds like sunflower seeds or cotton seeds are a key nourishment for livestock. They contain a lot of protein and energy and for that reason are the most used feedstuff for beef and dairy cows (Bernard 2016, 349–50). Demand for meat and dairy products in China increased sharply over the last decades because on the one hand more people can afford animal-based foods and on the other hand foreign dishes which contain more meat and dairy have become popular. Hence, meat consumption has skyrocketed from 7 million tons in 1975 to 75 million tons in 2016 (CSIS 2017). To feed the additional livestock 84 megatons of soybeans were imported by China in 2016. Because meat and dairy demand continues to rise it is expected that Chinese soybean imports will exceed 100 megatons by 2025. At the same time, global soybean exports are forecast to reach approximately 140 Megatons by 2025, which would mean that China would absorb around 70% of all soybean exports (Huang et al. 2017, 2939). Given the fact that 43,5% of current global soybean exports originate from the United States, China would not be able to import sufficient soybeans to feed all livestock without access to the US market - unless the market share of other soybean exporters increases drastically until 2025 (UN Comtrade 2018).

Table 45: Main exporters of soybeans

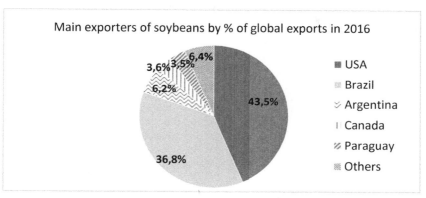

Source: (UN Comtrade 2018)

Replacing soybean and oilseeds with other feedstuff like maize, wheat or oats, which do not belong to product category grain, fruit and seeds (HS 12) but to cereals (HS 10), is no viable alternative, because the United States are also by far the biggest global exporter of cereals (UN Comtrade 2018).

Consequently, not only the food security for grain, fruit and seeds (HS 12) would be seriously endangered without access to the US market but also the meat and dairy production would be very negatively affected. While normally foodstuff is not a source of economic dependence, the special circumstances of demand and supply in certain food sectors make China dependent on imports of agricultural products from the United States.

Dependence on Imports

It is generally assumed that the United States depend more on imports from China than the other way around because China imports far less goods from the United States than the United States imports from China. In 2016 the difference was more than 300 billion US dollars (UN Comtrade 2018). However, the United States are still China's fourth most important import market and when it comes to imports that are consumed in China – and not re-exported - the United States might even come out on top. In this chapter it has been illustrated that more than one third of Chinese imports from its two most important import markets South Korea and Japan are intermediate goods which are ultimately re-exported. Since so-called processing imports are of lesser importance for the Chinese economy due to the relatively low aggregated value added of re-exports, this diminishes the significance of South Korea and Japan for import trade. Imports from the United States, by contrast, are to a larger part finished goods and designated for domestic consumption. The higher domestic consumption rate indicates that the majority of goods that China buys from the United States have a high significance for the Chinese economy. This assumption was confirmed in the chapter at hand:

- China spends most on imports of Advanced Technology Products from the product categories electrical equipment and electrical machinery (HS 85), machinery, engines and boilers (HS84), aircraft, spacecraft (HS 88) and optical, photographic, medical apparatus (HS 90).
- Despite high investments into research and development, China is still lacking know-how in many industries and must import many high-tech products which it cannot produce domestically – at least not in the near future.
- Some of the goods for which China has a high demand are high-end microchips, airplanes and medical devises. The United States are a key supplier for these products as 58,2% of all airplanes and 32,8% of medical devices come from the US. The market for some high-end microchips is even under complete control of US manufacturer.
- The aviation, medical technology and microchip sector are dominated by very few players which means that it is difficult to compensate the large amounts of airplanes, medical devices and microchips that China imports from the United and even if sufficient alternative supplies could be provided China would be in a very unfavourable situation towards the new suppliers because they would gain a quasi-monopoly for the Chinese market.
- Consequently, the vulnerability dependence is very high because imports from the United States can neither be adequately substituted with domestic production nor are sufficient alternative suppliers available to compensate imports without suffering shortages or less favourable market conditions.

As the majority of imports are high-tech products, which are vital to the Chinese economy, the costs of a disruption of trade with the United States would be high. A particularity of Chinese import dependence is that China would also suffer significant costs in the agricultural sector even though agricultural goods are generally seen as easily replaceable. However, the very high demand for food imports in conjunction with limitations to cultivation in China and the United States' market dominance for certain foodstuff results in a constellation in which Chinese food security would be threatened without imports from the United States. Thus, agricultural imports are also a source of considerable vulnerability dependence.

4.4.3   Chinese Trade Balance with the US

The bilateral trade balance has already been discussed in chapter 4.3.3. „US trade balance with China", but there are some aspects of it that need consideration from the Chinese side. It has also been elaborated in chapter 4.3.3. why trade balance in terms of exchanged goods between two economic territories is not a very meaningful measure anymore and can even be misleading, but it still is a good starting point for analysis. Therefore, the trade balance of exports and imports will also be the basis for the following discussion.

According to United States data on trade with China the American deficit in the trade balance was 366 billion US dollars in 2016. However, Chinese data on bilateral imports and exports only show a Chinese surplus of around 251 billion US dollars, which is 31,7% less than the American calculation. As has been explained before, trade data asymmetries do not result from incorrect national statistics but stem from different statistical approaches and a difference in partner country attribution for exports and imports; see chapter 4.1. It is peculiar that two very different trade balances exist which both are correct. This fact is very rarely discussed, but it has great political implications because depending on which country's data is used the evaluation of the trade balance differs. From a Chinese perspective the trade relationship is less unbalanced than from a US perspective. The existence of different trade balances casts further doubt on the usefulness of traditional trade statistics.

While in basically all international media only the American calculation of the Sino-American trade balance is discussed, Chinese media regularly highlight the discrepancy between US and Chinese trade data. The Chinese news agency Xinhua even went so far to call the US data "twisted" since it would inflate the US deficit (Xinhua News Agency 2018). Calling the data twisted is exaggerated since the United States does not purposefully use a statistical approach that results in a higher deficit and trade data asymmetries are a global phenomenon. Reported exports and imports very rarely correspond with reported imports and exports of a partner country though logically the exports of country A to country B should be the same as the imports of country A from country B. The Chinese critique is also misplaced because Chinese exports to the United States via Hong-Hong, which are declared as exports to Hong Kong by Chinese authorities but registered as imports from China by US authorities, make up a part of the difference in in trade balance. Shipments via intermediate countries should be declared as exports to the final destination because this is where the goods are consumed. Consequently, the Chinese trade balance should at least be adjusted for re-export from Hong Kong to the United States.

Table 46: Bilateral Trade Balance in Goods - US and China Data

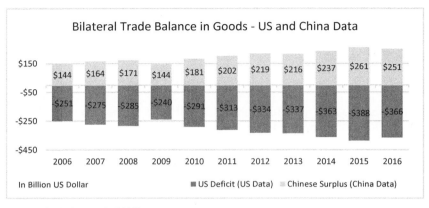

Source: (UN Comtrade 2018)

However, it is still worthwhile to consider that if the US statistical approach would differ the trade deficit would be only 251 billion US dollars, as calculated by the National Bureau of Statistics of China, and not 366 billion US dollars, as reported by the US Census Bureau. According to US data the trade deficit reached 251 billion US dollars in the year 2006 and in 2006 the trade deficit with China was not among the most pressing issues of US foreign policy. It stands to reason that less people in the United States would be worried about the US trade deficit if the US calculation of the deficit with China for 2016 would only be 251 billion US dollars, whereas a higher trade deficit makes it easier to gather support for actions against China. This might explain why President Trump wrongfully declared that the deficit would be as high as 500 billion US dollars (Trump 2018a).[9] The extent of the deficit has become a political tool in the United States.

Hence, it is understandable why from a Chinese perspective it looks like the trade relationship is not assessed objectively by the US government. This is problematic because not only is the extent of the trade deficit is debatable but also the validity of the number as an indicator for which country is benefitting more from the trade relationship is put into question. As has been explained in chapter 4.3.3 the United States profits more and China profits less from Sino-American business ties than traditional trade statistics suggest. If the foreign content of Chinese exports is subtracted and the revenue from

9   See chapter 4.3.3. for an explanation how Doanld Trump presumably came to the wrong
      conclusion that the trade deficit is 500 billion US dollars

US companies' operation within China is added to the trade balance than the trade relationship is close to balanced.

Furthermore, it must be considered that China invests a large part of the revenue from exports to the United States in US treasury securities and private securities. Since treasury securities are issued to finance US government spending, China basically loans money to the United States so that the US government can invest more into its own economy. By buying corporate securities and equities China provides new capital to American business, which is vital for economic expansion. Parts of the borrowed money will ultimately be used to buy more Chinese goods so that China in turn also profits when the United States can spend more (Beeson and Li 2015, 99). On the downside the United States piled up high debts with China that can become a liability. Borrowing itself is neither good nor bad, but it depends on how the borrowed money is spend. If the additional funding is only used on more consumption, borrowing from China will be unsustainable in the long run. However, if the money is used to stimulate the economy and to avoid other measures to increase public revenue that are contra-productive to economic development, like tax increases, then running into debt with China can be positive for the American economy (Lawrence 2018, 2).

As the US government continues to believe that it is necessary to take on debt in order to finance the public budget it is in need of lenders. China has the reserves to finance the US deficit and its high demand for US treasury securities has helped to keep interest rates low, from which the US government as well as private businesses profit (Oxford Economics 2017, 19). For as long as the US government continues the practice of deficit spending the United States can be pleased to have a reliable source of capital.

As of June 2017 China held US treasury securities worth 1,15 Trillion US dollars which is more than the holdings of any other country and equals 18,7% of all foreign holdings of US treasury securities (U.S. Department of the Treasury 2018a, B-9). Chinese holdings were even higher from 2012 until 2014 when China started to sell US treasury securities. However, since 2016 China restarted the acquisition and the holdings of treasury securities approaches the level of 2012 (Morrison 2018, 20). The foreign ownership of such a large share of American debts is worrisome to some financial analysts and politicians in the United States because they fear that China could use the financial obligations of the US government as leverage to influence American policy (Morrison 2018, 19–20). While it is true that China could cause serious financial and economic disturbances if it would sell large amounts of US treasury securities, such an action would be self-defeating because a weakening US economy would buy less Chinese goods and as has been shown in chapter 4.4.1 China depends on sales to the United States. Furthermore, large sales of US security treasuries would very likely devalue the dollars, which in turn would depreciate all remaining Chinese holdings in US dollars. A devaluation of Chinese financial reserve is unacceptable for the Chinese government because the money is needed to finance the enhancement of the Chinese economy following the "Made in China 2025" plan and to fund the countless infrastructure projects of the Belt and Road Initiative. A very unlikely scenario is that the United States decides not to repay its debts to China at all, but already the possibility of this scenario poses a risk for China. Therefore, the large holdings of US treasury securities is not only a concern to US politicians but is also discussed among Chinese elites. One of China's leadings government economists, Yu Yongding, justified the sales of US treasuries with the following quote, which is attributed to John Maynard Keynes.

"If you owe your bank manager a thousand pounds, you are at his mercy. If you owe him a million pounds, he is at your mercy." (The Economist 2009)

China lent so much money to the United States that it depends on repayment, which in turn creates an interdependence. The United States depend on capital from Beijing and China depends on a solvent US government and economy that can buy Chinese goods and repays its debts. Since the constellation is mutual beneficial and because opting out of this form of economic symbiosis would be painful for either side, both sides are incentivised to continue close economic cooperation.

5 Economic Incentives and Political Realities

The analysis has shown that economic interdependencies are strong across trade flows. The United States does not only depend on imports from China and China does not only depend on exports to the United States as is commonly assumed. While eastbound trade has a higher volume than westbound trade, shipments from the United States across the pacific are still very relevant for the US and Chinese economies alike.

They are important for the United States because China is the third largest export market for US products and projected to become the largest one by 2030. Furthermore, operations within China have become a major revenue source for many US companies and should be added to the export calculation. Westbound trade is important for China because the United States is the fourth largest import market for China and arguably the most important one for goods that are actually consumed in China and not only processed and re-exported. Furthermore, China is still reliant on the import of Advanced Technology Products, many of which it can only source from the United States, and China's enormous demand for food imports cannot be sufficiently satisfied without access to the United States because it is the world's largest agricultural commodity market.

By examining the composition of trade in detail it was revealed that a vast number of economic sectors are sensitive to disruptions in Sino-American economic interaction. A total of 21% of the United States' imports come from China and 8% of its exports go to China, while China satisfies 8,5% of its global import demand from the United States and exports 18,4% of its global output to the United States. Adjusting these enormous trade flows is difficult and finding alternative export and import markets is associated with high opportunity costs.

Some of the most vital economic sectors in the United States and China are even severely vulnerable to a discontinuation of trade ties. Import vulnerabilities are characterised by a market constellation in which a loss of imports cannot be sufficiently compensated by domestic production or alternative suppliers or only at lower quality or at a higher price. Export vulnerabilities are characterised by a situation in which a loss of an export market would lead to revenue losses because no sufficient alternative buyers are available or because the exported goods are customised and asset-specific.

The following economic sectors in the United States and China have been identified to have the most notable vulnerabilities:

United States

Import Vulnerabilities
- Smart phones and other communication devices
- Computer, laptops, tablets and servers
- Printer and other office machines
- Monitors and projectors
- Rare-earth metals and rare-earth products

Export Vulnerabilities[10]
- Aircraft (Boeing)
- Cars (GM, Ford, Chrysler)
- Microchips (Skyworks, Qualcomm, Broadcom, Nvidia)
- Food Service Industry (YUM Brands, Starbucks, McDonalds)
- Grain, fruit and seeds including soya beans

China

Import Vulnerabilities
- High-end microchips (GPUs, MPUs)
- Aircraft
- Medical devices
- Agricultural products

Export Vulnerabilities
- Computers, laptops, tablets and servers
- Smart phones and other communication devices
- Mechanical appliances
- Furniture
- Clothing
- Toys and games
- Sport requisites

The analysis of business ties across economic sectors has revealed that trade in goods is only one dimension of economic interaction. The business activities of American companies in China and Chinese companies in the United States account for large parts of company revenues and several US companies already make more profit with operations in China than with exports to China. The largest US microchip producers have a revenue exposure to China between 36% and 83%. Much of this revenue comes from licence fees and royalties rather than exports; see page 67. This aspect of economic interaction is easily overlooked as the profits which US and Chinese companies realise

10   Including vulnerabilities from business activities within China (revenue exposure)

across the pacific are not included in trade balance data. Given the importance of foreign business operations, vulnerabilities stemming from revenue exposure have also been added to export vulnerabilities.

It is not surprising that for some economic sectors one country's export vulnerabilities are the other country's import vulnerabilities. If country A is a large buyer of a product from country B this means the trade volume is so high that country B will probably be one of the major sources of this product for country A. If country B is also one of the largest suppliers of this good worldwide and country A is one of the largest buyers worldwide, then country A has few alternatives to source this product and country B has few alternatives to sell this product. As both countries could not substitute all exports or all imports respectively, they are vulnerable to a discontinuation of bilateral trade exchange.

Such a constellation exists, for example, in the aviation industry. China is the largest buyer of US aircrafts and the United States is China's largest supplier. Since the United States is also one of the largest aircraft producers in the world and China is one of the largest aircraft buyers in the world, the United States runs the risk not to sell all aircrafts and China runs the risk to receive less aircrafts than it needs if one side decides to end the cooperation. Thus, the aviation industry is a source of mutual vulnerability because the United States can hurt China and China can hurt the United States, but neither can do so without hurting themselves. The same is true for the computer/laptop industry and the smartphone industry where China-based Original Design Manufacturer/Original Equipment Manufacturer depend on US retailers and the other way around. Other economic sectors that are mutually vulnerable include microchips and some parts of the agricultural sector with the soya bean industry being the prime example.

There are also economic sectors where the vulnerabilities are unilateral. In export industries this happens when country A exports large volumes of a product to country B and has no sufficient alternative buyers to sell all its production, but country B has sufficient alternative sources for this product and can satisfy its demand without country A. In this constellation country A is unilaterally vulnerable to country B. An example for a unilaterally vulnerable export sector is the US automotive industry. US car manufacturer are vulnerable to a ban from the Chinese market because nobody else would by the cars that US manufacturers can no longer sell in China, but China can instead buy cars from other countries with a large automotive industry like Germany, Japan, France or Italy or even produce more cars domestically to satisfy its demand. The clothing business is an example for a Chinese export industry that is unilaterally vulnerable.

Unilateral vulnerabilities also exist for imports if country A imports large volumes of a product from country B and has no sufficient alternative suppliers to satisfy its demand, but country B has sufficient alternative buyers so that it could stop sales to country A without losing revenue. In this constellation country A is unilaterally vulnerable to country B. This is the case for high-tech industries in the United States, which are vulnerable to a cut-off from rare-earth metal imports from China because no sufficient alternative suppliers exist, but since the demand for rare-earth metals is globally rising, China could probably find sufficient alternative buyers elsewhere in the world.

Global supply chains reinforce vulnerabilities because they intertwine business sectors to a point where dependencies can only be unravelled at high costs and in case of less diversified supply chains, where only a few and sometimes even just one supplier produces a necessary component, they cannot be unravelled at all. The case of ZTE has been discussed as an example of a company that was close to a shutdown as a result of a cut-off from US microchip suppliers; see chapter 4.4.2. Apple is another example for the impact of supply chains because the company relies on production in China and can hardly shift supply chains; see chapter 4.3.2.1. Throughout chapter four many more examples of businesses sectors intertwined by supply chains have been discussed. Thanks to the outsourcing of production and a global division of labour there is hardly any industry in which the United States and China are not involved in the supply chain. Thus, no economic sector can be shielded from the negative consequences of a discontinuation of economic relations.

As has been discussed in chapter 2.1, symmetry is a precondition for the effectiveness of economic interdependencies. While asymmetric interdependence might cause jealousies and can result in rivalry, symmetric interdependence causes mutual gains and incentivises continued cooperation. When mutual vulnerabilities and unilateral vulnerabilities between the United States and China are added up and weighted against each other, the result is a fairly symmetrical interdependence. A disruption in trade relations would result in equally painful losses and cause very high opportunity costs for both economies. Also, the trade balance is much more equal if the composition of trade is examined in more detail and if not only the exchange in physical goods is considered. China exports significantly more to the United States than the United States export to China, but not every export is a gain for the exporting nation. An iPhone that is assembled in China and exported to the United States increases the US trade deficit but since it is ultimately sold by a US company it also increases the American GDP. Furthermore, as has been discussed in chapter 4.3.3 and 4.4.3., the United States profits more from economic exchange than trade statistics reveal because of the revenue from activities within China. And China profits less from trade with the United States because a large part of exports are re-exports with low value added in China. Consequently, it can be concluded that gains are evenly distributed, which means there is no incentive to cancel cooperation based on the assumption that one country is on the losing side.

Since interdependence is symmetric and not only very high in terms of sensitivities but also in the form of very strong vulnerabilities for many economic sectors, the incentive for continued cooperation is very high. In addition, both sides are not just encouraged to preserve economic ties out of fear for negative consequences, but it also became apparent in the analysis of economic interactions that Sino-American economic cooperation results in mutual gains. Thanks to lower production costs in China, goods can be imported at a cheap price which profits US consumers and increases US companies' profit margins and competitiveness. China, on the other side, generates jobs and revenue from production for the US market. Chapter 4.4.1. discussed the high contribution that Chinese exports to the United States have for the economic development of the Chinese economy. Economic ties with China are also an important factor for the economic performance of the United States and since China is one of very few markets that still have a high growth potential continued cooperation with China offers many opportunities for US businesses to expand their operations; see chapter 4.3.2. Hence, the assumptions of Immanuel Kant and Adam Smith that a maximum of prosperity can only be achieved through free trade and cooperation prove to be true for US-China relations.

These findings support the hypothesis that was derived from the US-China relationship model. It was theorised in chapter 3 that economic interdependence increases the costs of defection and the payoffs of cooperation for the United States and China. As has been proven, the losses for choosing defection are very high for both countries due to high sensitivity vulnerabilities across business sectors and the large amount of strong mutual and unliteral vulnerabilities. At the same increasing the interconnectedness of the US and Chinese economy, thereby fostering interdependencies, led to positive effects for both countries and increased the payoffs of cooperation. Consequently, there is a high incentive for the United States as well as China not to defect from cooperation by introducing more confrontational policies but to continue cooperation in order avoid the negative consequences of a conflict and to preserve the mutual gain of economic exchange.

While the analysis of Sino-American economic exchange revealed that the high level of economic interdependence encourages both sides to continue cooperation, economic incentive alone might not be enough to prevent a confrontation altogether. Recent events show that despite major downsides, the US and China engaged in a costly trade dispute. This raises the question why economic incentives failed to prevent the dispute?

One explanation comes from commercial liberalism theory itself. The Nobel Peace Prize winner Norman Angell was convinced of the pacifying effect of trade but came to realise at the beginning of the 20th century that statesmen still cherished the "great illusion" of power politics. He criticised politicians for their assumption that "territorial expansion and exercise of political force against others" would still be the best way to achieve prosperity and wealth for their people (Angell 2013, 299). He referred to the commercial success of smaller and less powerful nations like Belgium, Swiss and Norway as evidence for his assumptions. His argument is that due to advanced communication technology and international financial markets, property and wealth have become intangible in great part. Thus, it has become

"impossible for one nation to seize by force the wealth or trade of another [...]. War, even when victorious, can no longer achieve those aims for which people strive." (Angell 2013, 300)

However, Angell was aware that this rationale was not yet recognised by all politicians. In fact, he was even ridiculed by politicians for his theory that war had become economically self-defeating. Therefore, he expected that wars would not end until the predominant basic assumptions about international politics, economic cooperation and the wealth of nations would change. Angell was convinced that the Anglo-German rivalry and armament, which preceded the First World War, could have been overcome by a change of attitude towards war and free trade (Angell 2013, 301). He is not the only one who argued that European politicians had misunderstood the mechanisms of economic interdependence and misperceived the costs of war in the run up to the First World War (Gartzke and Lupu 2012, 121).

It is logical that economic interdependence only constrains people when they realise the opportunity costs of conflict and accept to work within its limits. If economic interdependencies are misperceived or not taken into consideration at all, they will not have an impact on political relations (Rosecrance 2013, 357). Thus, one explanation for the US-China trade conflict is that the current US government is not realising the extent to which the US economy depends on China and how vulnerable many economic sectors are.

Another explanation is that China and the United States are not only trading partners, but also economic and political competitors. Depending on how each side evaluates this competition, one might come to different assessment of US-China relations. Competition can either be seen as necessity of a liberal international system and positive stimulus for countries to make an effort to keep improving oneself. Or it can be seen as threat to its own position in the international system and risk for the well-being of its national economy. Americans have to ask themselves: do we accept that China might come out on top of the competition, surpassing the United States in terms of economic output and political influence? Someone who answers "no" to this question will view competition with China fundamentally different than someone who answers "yes" to this question. Vice versa Chinese have to ask themselves:

do we accept that the US might comes out on top of the competition and continues to exceed China in economic output and political influence. Someone who answers "no" to this question might be willing to play unfair and risk a confrontation with the United States.

If winning the competition and becoming or remaining the world's most powerful nation is the number one priority, then suffering the negative consequences of an economic conflict might be acceptable as long as this helps the cause and hurts the competitor more than oneself. Thus, it is possible that someone who is fully aware of the negative consequences can still start a conflict with an interdependent trading partner. This argument has already been made in more detail in the discussion of the causal mechanics of interdependence in chapter 2.1.

Nevertheless, also someone who is willing to suffer negative consequences will be influenced by economic incentives in their decision making. The higher the incentive, the more difficult the decision to risk the economic stability of a country. Furthermore, if it is not possible to cause bigger loses to the competitor than oneself would suffer from a trade conflict, then it would even be more logical for someone who only thinks in relative gains to continue cooperation because this way the relative power decline will be smaller. In a relationship of symmetrical interdependence causing higher losses to a trading partner than to oneself is near impossible as vulnerabilities are mutual. As long as the competitor is willing to retaliate, there is little chance of winning an advantage from a confrontation. Thus, economic interdependence remains relevant in already conflictual relationships as it continues to exert a positive effect on decision making and because it reduces the possibilities to win a trade conflict.

From the above can be concluded that the human factor is incredibly important for the effectiveness of economic interdependence. Symmetric economic interdependencies will always exert an incentive for cooperation, but how much someone is taking economic factors into consideration depends on their understanding of economic interactions and their assessment of the political situation. Consequently, it is decisive who the decision makers in Beijing and Washington are and how they asses the bilateral economic and well as political relations. For that reason, the next chapter will examine the human factor in US-China relations.

6 The Human Factor in US-China Relations

Past statements and proposals by high officials on both sides suggest that economic rationale have had a meaningful effect on US-China relations in the past. In a private conversation between then-Secretary of State Hilary Clinton and then-Prime Minister of Australia Kevin Rudd, which has been transcribed by the US State Department and made public by WikiLeaks, Clinton expressed her concern about the challenges posed by China's economic rise, asking, "how do you deal toughly with your banker?" (WikiLeaks 2009).

This quote illustrates two thinks: First, Hilary Clinton acknowledged America's dependence on China in terms of government debts, which is an important aspect of Sino-American economic independence. One might argue that this is a highly asymmetrical constellation, but in fact it is symmetrical as has been explained in chapter 4.4.3. If the US would choose not to repay its debts, China would suffer high losses as well.

Second, Clinton implies that the US was not "dealing toughly" with China - at least during her time in office - meaning that the US policy on China was less confrontational as it would have been in absence of economic dependencies. This is an important and very concrete indication that US foreign policy towards China has been influenced by economic considerations.

On the Chinese side such a straightforward quote is not available, but President Xi Jinping's proposal for a "new type of great power relations" between China and the US in 2013 tells much about the Chinese understanding of the relationship. When Xi considers it necessary to develop a new "new type" of great power relations he must have, as a first step, realised that the "old" or existing types of great power relations are inadequate and that competition between established and rising powers is potentially dangerous. Therefore, the former president of the China Institutes of Contemporary International Relations, Cui Liru, believes the proposition of a "new type of great power relations" is intended as a mechanism to prevent hostilities and preserve cooperation (Cui 2013 et. al.).

Since the election of Donald Trump, the political dynamic has changed and China is no longer perceived primarily as an economic partner by the United States but as a competitor and challenger. The following quote from Trump's book "Crippled America. How to Make America Great Again", has an aggressive tone and paints the picture of a China that is deliberately hurting the US economy:

"There are people who wish I wouldn't refer to China as our enemy. But that's exactly what they are. They have destroyed entire industries by utilizing low-wage workers, cost us tens of thousands of jobs, spied on our businesses, stolen our technology, and have manipulated and devalued their currency, which makes importing our goods more expensive – and sometimes, impossible." (Trump 2015)

If Donald Trump actually sees China as an enemy and suspects hostile intentions, this could explain why he is prepared to confront China despite negative consequences for the United States economy. Furthermore, the quote lacks any acknowledgement of benefits for the United States from economic interactions with China. If Donald Trump views trade with China only as liability and denies any gains for the United States, he will not be restrained out of fear over economic losses. That Donald Trump is unaware of the extent of the economic interdependencies and the costs of a trade conflict with China is illustrated in a twitter post from 2018 that preceded the introduction of tariffs on Chinese exports:

"When a country (USA) is losing many billions of dollars on trade with virtually every country it does business with, trade wars are good, and easy to win." (Trump 2018b)

The assessment that trade wars can be won is based on the assumption that the United States is benefitting less from trade relations than their partner countries. As has been discussed in chapter 2.1, unfair trade relations can encourage a country to confront a trading partner in order to achieve more favourable trade conditions as long as the partner would lose more from a conflict. If the United States would actually "lose many billions of dollars on trade" with China, then it would make sense to put the economic relationship at risk to alter the conditions. However, it has been proven in this study that the gains from economic interaction are mutual and roughly balanced. Thus, the United States have as much to lose from a trade war as China. Due to the deep vulnerabilities on both side the United States can hardly take any measures without hurting its own economy. Tariffs are a double-edged sword in economic sectors with mutual vulnerabilities. The United States could only introduce tariffs or non-tariff measures in economic sectors with unilateral vulnerabilities for China, but China could easily retaliate with tariffs and non-tariff measures in economic sectors with unilateral vulnerabilities for the United States. If no side is giving in, a trade war between countries with strong symmetrical interdependencies cannot be won. That President Trump thinks trade wars are easy to win reveals his denial of the United States' dependence on economic interaction with China. A misperception of economic relations and US vulnerabilities would explain why Donald Trump started a trade conflict with China.

Despite labelling China as "enemy" and his assumption that the United States have less to lose from a trade conflict, he seems not totally committed to a confrontation. The beginning of his presidency featured meetings and phone calls with the Chinese President Xi Jinping that were perceived as constructive and friendly in tone. This was a harsh contrast to Trump's China bashing during his campaign and at odds with the promise to deal tough with China (The Economist 2017). It seemed as if President Trump was rather interested in striking a deal with China to increase the gains from economic interaction than to drag China into a trade war to keep China down. Even after relations cooled off and the prospects for a deal dropped, President Trump waited a long time before he rolled out full-fledged tariffs on Chinese exports in July 2018. The gradual expansion of the tariff list over the next months also looks more like a strategy to bring China back to the negotiation table than as an attempt to contain China's economic growth. This interpretation of the goal behind the trade conflict is supported by comments President Trump made about the development of trade negotiations:

"When the time is right we will make a deal with China. My respect and friendship with President Xi is unlimited but, as I have told him many times before, this must be a great deal for the United States or it just doesn't make any sense. We have to be allowed to make up some of the tremendous ground we have lost to China on trade (…)." (Trump 2019)

His desire to achieve a deal suggests that President Trump would like to continue cooperation with China. While he states the United States would have "lost ground", he probably realises the merit for the US economy or otherwise it would not make sense to push so hard for trade negotiations. If he would be absolutely convinced that the United States is not dependent on China and does not profit from economic exchange, then cutting trade ties completely would be the logical step. As he is not doing so but instead aims at a settlement this means that economic incentives are taken into consideration and while there is an apparent misperception of the extent of economic interdependencies and their effects on the US economy, they still have an influence on negotiations.

Economic interdependence also influences the US decision making through internal pressure. As the negative consequences of tariffs on Chinese exports start to have an ever greater impact on the US economy, it is no longer just farmers who request to settle the trade conflict but the business community as a whole is becoming increasingly worried and dissatisfied with President Trump (The Economist 2019a). Also within the republican party critique of the trade dispute increases as a series of senators, primarily from states with a large farming industry, voiced their opposition to a continuation of the trade conflict (Financial Times 2019).

China tries to exploit this internal pressure and introduced counter-tariffs on goods like soya beans for which the United States have export vulnerabilities. At the same time the Chinese tariffs particularly target those states which have a large Trump supporter basis (The Economist 2019c). Such targeted measures are only possible because economic interdependencies are strong and make the US economy vulnerable to changes in trade relations with China.

7 Conclusion

The combined quantitative and qualitative analysis of economic interactions between the United States and China generated new insights in what makes countries become interdependent and how economic interdependencies effect political relations. It was shown that it is not just important how much is being trade but what is being trade has a decisive impact on economic interdependence. While the trade volume is a good indicator for how sensitive a country is towards changes in its trade relations, only the composition of trade determines how vulnerable a country is towards a discontinuation of trade ties with a partner country. Furthermore, it was demonstrated that trade in physical goods is still a major part of economic exchange, but it is not the only dimension of economic interaction anymore and thus it is also not the only source of interdependencies anymore. How important economic relations really are is increasingly determined by the extent of business activities within a foreign country. US companies produce less and less at home, which is why the United States export muss less goods to China than other way around, but instead American companies make revenue with foreign subsidies, joint-ventures, license-fees and other forms of business activities.

Consequently, it is not enough to assess traditional trade statistics which only measure the exchange of goods to determine the extent of economic interdependencies. In fact, trade statistics can be misleading and it was demonstrated that the way bilateral trade is measured in international statistics results in a distorted assessment of economic relations between the United States and China. When only the sum of imports and exports, i.e. the bilateral trade balance, is considered, then economic interactions seem to favour China as it has a large trade surplus towards the United States. However, this study has illustrated that the trade balance in exchanged goods is not a meaningful indicator for the extent that a country benefits from economic interaction and the Chinese trade surplus does not mean China is more dependent on trade relations than the United States. Chinese exports to the United States contain a lot of foreign components but China only profits from the value that has been added in China. If only the value added in exchanged goods is measured, the Chinese trade surplus shrinks by approximately 35%. Furthermore, it must be taken into account that many foreign firms shifted production to China and as a consequence now export goods from China to the United States. The exports from foreign firms who produce in China contribute to the Chinese trade surplus but China profits only partially from these exports. Also, moving production from countries like Japan, South Korea, Singapore, or Hong-Hong to China results in a change of the trade balance between these countries and the United States in favour of the latter. Thus, parts of the Chinese trade surplus with the United States are redirected surpluses of other countries. If these factors are taken together, it becomes obvious that China profits far less from exports to the United States than the trade surplus suggests.

At the same time the United States profits not only from exports to China but also from imports from China because a considerably amount of goods that are shipped from China to the United States are in fact outsourced production of US companies. Thanks to cheaper production costs in China, US companies have a higher revenue margin and are more competitive. Furthermore, if US companies produce in China, their shipments to the United States will increase the US trade deficit but as the sales of the imported products increase the revenue of US companies, the US economy actually profits from these imports. Furthermore, any revenue that is generated through operations of US companies in China is not included in the trade balance. Not including business activities in the trade balance distorts data in favour of China because for many US companies the revenue from business activities exceeds the revenue from exports. The trade balance becomes more equal when it is adjusted for the factors which decrease China's benefits and which increase the United States' benefits. As has been discussed in chapter 4.3.3, some calculations even suggest the United States profits more from economic interactions than China.

A correct calculation of how much a country benefits from economic exchange is essential in order to determine the influence of economic interdependence. Countries are interdependent because they generate gains from cooperation and would lose those gains if cooperation is stopped. If one country benefits more, interdependence becomes asymmetric as the country who benefits less has less to lose. The more asymmetric the interdependence between two countries, the less it incentivises cooperation. As the United States and China benefit roughly equally from economic exchange, the economic interdependence is symmetric and incentivises both countries to continue cooperation.

The level of incentive depends on the strength of economic interdependence and the strength of economic interdependence depends on each country's sensitivities and vulnerabilities to a discontinuation of bilateral trade ties. The detailed analysis of trade flows, composition of trade and other economic activities revealed a very high sensitivity interdependence across all economic sectors and very deep vulnerabilities for several important industries in the United States and China. The United States is especially vulnerable to measures that would prevent the import of smart phones, computers, printers, monitors and rare-earth metals from China, while China is vulnerable to a discontinuation of imports in high-end microchips, aircrafts, medical devices and certain agricultural products from the United States. US industries with serious vulnerabilities to export restrictions include the aircraft industry, car manufacturer, microchip producers, the food service industry, and parts of the agricultural sector. Chinese industries with serious vulnerabilities to export restrictions include computer and smartphones manufacturer, furniture companies, the clothing industry, and producers of toys and sport requisites.

The above listed industries support thousands of jobs and contribute greatly to the GDP of the United States and China. Some of the vulnerable sectors like car manufacturing in the United States or computer producer in China are considered core industries of their countries and are essential for the economic performance of the United States and China, respectively. Sectors that include Advanced Technology Products like smart phones, microchips or aircrafts also have a strategic importance for the United States and China. Consequently, any damage to these industries would have serious consequences, which is why vulnerabilities cannot easily be ignored and exert a very high incentive on both sides to continue peaceful and cooperative relations.

While economic interdependence highly incentivises both sides to avoid a confrontation, this study also discussed the limitations of economic interdependence and possible reasons why economic interdependence did to prevent the US and China to engage in a trade conflict. One explanation for a dispute between interdependent countries is that political leader misperceives the extent and consequences of economic interdependence. Another explanation is that political leaders can accept to suffer the economic costs of a conflict with an interdependent partner in order to achieve a political goal like geopolitical predominance. However, such a strategy that weaponises economic interdependence is only rational if the partner country would suffer higher costs from an economic dispute than oneself. In a constellation of symmetric economic interdependence both countries suffer the same from a discontinuation of economic interaction, which makes winning a trade dispute only possible if the partner country does not retaliate to the same extent.

Statements President Trump made regarding US economic ties with China suggest that he misperceives how much the United States profits from the economic relationship. Consequently, he underestimates the negative consequences of a prolonged trade dispute with China as is apparent from his assessment that "trade wars are good, and easy to win" (Trump 2018b). A miscalculation of the economic constellation would explain why the US administration arrived at the conclusion that starting a trade dispute would be advantageous to the United States. However, the US president seems at least to some degree constrained by economic considerations. While his rhetoric is harsh and confrontational, calling China as an "enemy", he shows no intention to stop economic interaction altogether, but on the contrary wants to achieve better market access for US companies. US diplomacy towards China, while more aggressive than under previous administrations, still showed a considerable level of restraint since tariffs were only introduced after several round of negotiations and only gradually increased. This behaviour suggests that the goal of the trade dispute is not to contain China but to pressure Beijing into a deal that would allow the US to continue cooperation at more favourable terms. While President Trump does not acknowledge the full extent of economic interdependence between the United States and China, there are reasons to believe he realises the stakes are high, wants to limit the negative consequences for the US economy and would like to preserve the gains of cooperation. Since the US economy already started to suffer from the trade dispute with China, the president is also pressured by business leaders, politicians from both parties and not least from voters to settle the dispute. Thus, economic interdependence, albeit not enough to prevent a dispute, has a positive influence on US-China relations and on the development of negotiations.

In the long run, it would be possible for the United States to reduce vulnerabilities and become less dependent to China. That could increase the political leeway to "deal more toughly with China", to put it into the words of Hilary Clinton, without having to fear very severe consequences for the US economy. However, it was demonstrated in this study that unravelling economic interdependencies is difficult, results in high opportunity costs and has long term disadvantages for the US economy. The costs of achieving a status of considerable economic independence from China make such efforts economically undesirable. It is also questionable if decoupling the United States and China is politically desirable. During the 2019 Shangri-La Dialogue the Singaporean defense minister Ng Eng Hen addressed the cooling relationship between the United States and China and warned that:

"Shifting economic dependencies could lead to parallel blocs with strong divisions between them, setting countries up for conflict. So we're very clear what's at stake and we want to maintain the current system. We still believe that multilateral trade arrangements are not only important for economic dependencies and for economic health, but indeed, for security. Because if I trade a lot with you, it's quite hard for me to fight with you." (Ng Eng Hen 2019)

Indeed, breaking up interdependencies and creating isolated trade blocs could reverse the incentive and not restrain countries from conflict but encourage them to challenge each other as the negative economic effects of a conflict would be small.

Former Secretary of the Treasure Henry M. Paulson Jr. made a similar warning that attempts to decouple the United States and China could ultimately lead to an "economic iron curtain" that would not only separate the two countries and increase competition to a point where the United States and China could become adversaries. An economic separation would also deeply hurt the US economy as it would partly de-integrate the United States from the global economy by excluding US companies from global supply chains and international technology innovations that include China (Paulson 2019).

Thus, reducing interdependencies with China has many negative implications for the United States and it is doubtful if it would change the political power constellation in the United States' favour. It would also set a dangerous precedence if the two most important economic powers in the world would decide to de-integrate their economies. Other countries could follow the example and also try to reduce their dependencies on partner countries. This could have devastating consequences not only for the world economy but also for international security. As economic interdependencies make conflicts less desirable for everybody, business links between countries should be fostered and not cut back. Any attempts by political leaders to de-integrate their countries from the world economy would make world politics more insecure and increase the prospects of economic disputes.

8 Bibliography

Aero. 2018. "Handelskrieg Gibt Airbus Rückenwind in China." Aviation Media. 2018. https://www.aero.de/news-29419/Kann-Airbus-in-China-an-Boeing-vorbei ziehen.html.

Aerotelegraph. 2015. "Nun Beglückt China Auch Airbus." 2015. https://www.aero telegraph.com/nun-beglueckt-china-auch-airbus.

Akyüz, Yilmaz. 2011. "Export Dependence and Sustainability of Growth in China." *China & World Economy* 19 (1): 1–23.

Allison, Graham. 2015. "Thucydides Trap Case File." Belfer Center for Science and International Affairs. 2015. https://www.belfercenter.org/thucydides-trap/over view-thucydides-trap.

AmCham China. 2017. "2017 AmCham China White Paper." Beijing.

American Soybean Association. 2018. "U.S. Soybean Producers." 2018. https://soygrowers.com/.

Angell, Norman. 2013. "The Great Illusion: A Study of the Relation of Military Power and National Advantage." In *Conflict after the Cold War: Arguments on Causes of War and Peace*, edited by Richard K. Betts. Boston.

Apple. 2017. "Annual Report 2017." http://files.shareholder.com/downloads/AAPL/0x0x962680/D18FAEFF-460A-4168-993D-A60CBA8ED209/_10-K_2017_As-Filed_.pdf.

— 2018a. "Apple Accelerates US Investment and Job CreationTitle." https://www.apple.com/newsroom/2018/01/apple-accelerates-us-investment-and-job-creation/.

— 2018b. "Supplier List." https://www.apple.com/supplier-responsibility/pdf/Apple-Supplier-List.pdf.

Assche, Ari Van. 2012. *Global Value Chains and Canada's Trade Policy: Business as Usual or Paradigm Shift? IRPP Study.* http://irpp.org/wp-content/uploads/assets/research/competitiveness/global-value-chains-and-canadas-trade-policy/IRPP-Study-no32.pdf.

BEA. 2017. "Activities of U. S. Multinational Enterprises in 2015." https://apps.bea.gov/scb/pdf/2017/12-December/1217-activities-of-us-multinational-enterprises.pdf.

Beeson, Mark, and Fujian Li. 2015. "What Consensus? Geopolitics and Policy Paradigms in China and the United States." *International Affairs* 91 (1). https://doi.org/10.1111/1468-2346.12188.

Bernard, John K. 2016. "Oilseed and Oilseed Meals." In *Reference Module in Food Science*. Amsterdam: Elsevier. https://doi.org/http://doi.org/10.1016/B978-0-08-100596-5.00756-3.

Bieler, Andreas, and Chun-Yi Lee. 2017. *Chinese Labour in the Global Economy - Capitalist Exploitation and Strategies of Resistance.* New York: Routledge.

Bijian, Zheng. 2005. "China's 'Peaceful Rise' to Great-Power Status." *Foreign Affairs* 84 (5): 18–24. https://doi.org/10.2307/20031702.

Blackwill, Roberto D., and Kurt M Campbell. 2016. "Xi Jinping on the Global Stage." *Council on Foreign Relations Special Report.*

Blainey, George. 2013. "Paradise Is a Bazaar." In *Conflict after the Cold War: Arguments on Causes of War and Peace*, edited by Richard K. Betts. Boston: Pearson.

Blanchard, Jean-Marc F., and Norrin M. Ripsman. 1996. "Measuring Economic Interdependence: A Geopolitical Perspective." *Geopolitics and International Boundaries* 1 (3): 225–46. https://doi.org/10.1080/13629379608407567.

Boeing. 2017. "Current Market Outlook 2017-2036." http://www.boeing.com/ resources/boeingdotcom/commercial/market/current-market-outlook-2017/assets/downloads/cmo-2018-3-20.pdf.

Bombardier. 2017. "CRJ 1000 - Fact Sheet." http://commercialaircraft.bombardier. com/themes/bca/pdf/FactSheet_CRJ_Series_CRJ1000.pdf.

Brandt, Reinhard. 2011. "Vom Weltbürgertum." In *Immanuel Kant: Zum Ewigen Frieden*, edited by Otfried Höffe, 3rd ed., 220. Berlin: Akademie Verlag GmbH.

Buzan, Barry. 2004. *The United States and Great Powers*. Cambridge: Polity.

Cain, Peter. 1979. "Capitalism, War and Internationalism in the Thought of Richard Cobden." *British Journal of International Studies* 5 (03): 229. https://doi.org/ 10.1017/s0260210500114834.

CAPA. 2018. "Record Global Aircraft Deliveries in 2017: Boeing Ahead of Airbus Again, but behind on Order Backlog | CAPA." CAPA - Center for Aviation. 2018. https://centreforaviation.com/analysis/reports/record-global-aircraft-deliveries-in-2017-boeing-ahead-of-airbus-again-but-behind-on-order-backlog-393914.

CCCMHPIE. 2017. "Import Statistics of China's Medical Devices 2016." Trade Statistics. 2017. http://en.cccmhpie.org.cn/Web/Second.aspx?PClassID=49& ClassID=61.

China Daily. 2015. "Ministry Unveils Blueprint to Boost Manufacturing." *China Daily*, 2015. http://usa.chinadaily.com.cn/epaper/2015-05/20/content_20772187. htm.

China Freight Broker. 2016. "Transit Time Finder for China Freight." 2016. https:// cargofromchina.com/transit-time/.

China Med Device. 2018. "Trump Tariffs Will Hurt U.S. Medtech Companies More." 2018. https://chinameddevice.com/trump-tariffs-on-china-will-hurt-us-medtech-companies-more-or-not/.

China State Council. 2018. "The Facts and China's Position on China-US Trade Friction." Beijing. http://english.scio.gov.cn/whitepapers/2018-09/25/content_ 63998615.htm.

Chinese Central Government. 2009. "Full Text of Chinese Premier Wen Jiabao's Speech at 2009 Summer Davos in Dalian." The Chinese Central Government's Official Web Portal. 2009. http://www.gov.cn/english/2009-09/11/content_ 1414917.htm.

Chu, Yun-han. 2013. "Sources of Regime Legitimacy and the Debate over the Chinese Model." *China Review* 13 (1): 1–42.

Cobden, Richard. 1903. *The Political Writings of Richard Cobden, Vol. 1*. 4th ed. London: T. Fisher Unwin.

Compal Electronics. 2013. "Compal AEP Introduction." Taipei. http://micropac.it/wp-content/uploads/2016/11/COMPAL.pdf.

— 2018. "2017 Annual Report." Taipei. http://www.compal.com/mediafiles/sh-meeting/annual-report/2017_ENG_Annual_Report_Compal_FINAL.pdf.

Cooper, Richard N. 1968. *The Economics of Interdependence: Economic Policy in the Atlantic Community*. New York: McGraw-Hill.

CSIS. 2017. "How Is China Feeding Its Population of 1.4 Billion?" China Power. 2017. https://chinapower.csis.org/china-food-security/.

Cumings, Bruce. 2005. *Korea's Place in the Sun: A Modern History*. New York: Norton & Company.

Daiwa Security Group. 2016. "Lenovo Revenue Analysis." http://asiaresearch. daiwacm.com/eg/cgi-bin/files/20160818cn_Lenovo_Group.pdf.

Dell. 2017. "Dell Supplier List October 2017." https://i.dell.com/sites/doccontent/ corporate/corp-comm/en/Documents/dell-suppliers.pdf?newtab=true.

Descartes Datamyne. 2018. "HTS Code 8471 Automatic Data Processing Machines And Units Thereof; Magnetic Or Optical Readers, Machines For Transcribing And Processing Coded Data, Others." 2018. http://www.datamyne.com/hts/84/ 8471.

Dorussen, Han. 2006. "Heterogeneous Trade Interests and Conflict." *Journal of Conflict Resolution* 50 (1): 87–107.

Erickson, Andrew S., and Adam P. Liff. 2014. "Not-So-Empty Talk - The Danger of China's 'New Type of Great-Power Relations' Slogan." *Foreign Affairs*, October. https://www.foreignaffairs.com/articles/china/2014-10-09/not-so-empty -talk.

Feenstra, Robert, and Gordon Hanson. 2004. "Intermediaries in Entrepot Trade: Hong Kong Re-Exports of Chinese Goods." *Journal of Economics & Management Strategy* 13 (1): 3–35.

Ferguson, Niall, and Moritz Schularick. 2007. "'Chimerica' and the Global Asset Market Boom." *International Finance* 10 (3): 215–39. https://doi.org/10.1111/j. 1468-2362.2007.00210.x.

— 2011. "The End of Chimerica." *International Finance* 14 (1): 1–26. https://doi. org/10.1111/j.1468-2362.2010.01274.x.

Ferguson, Niall, and Xiang Xu. 2018. "Making Chimerica Great Again." *International Finance* 21 (3): 239–52. https://doi.org/10.1111/infi.12335.

Financial Times. 2019. "Trump's China Trade Policies Create Split among Republicans." 2019. https://www.ft.com/content/d2f2bf62-75c1-11e9-be7d-6d84 6537acab.

Forbes Magazine. 2018. "How Much Would An IPhone Cost If Apple Were Forced To Make It In America?" *Forbes Magazine*, 2018. https://www.forbes.com/sites/ quora/2018/01/17/how-much-would-an-iphone-cost-if-apple-were-forced-to-make-it-in-america/#173c4b602d2a.

Foxconn. 2016. "Annual Report 2016." http://www.foxconn.com/Files/annual_rpt_e/ 2016_annual_rpt_e.pdf.

Friedman, Thomas L. 2005. *The World Is Flat: A Brief History of the Globalized World in the 21st Century*. London: Allen Lane.

Fuchs, Martina. 2011. "Risiken Weltweiter Wertschöpfungsketten." No. 2011-01. http://www.wigeo.uni-koeln.de/sites/wigeo/Veroeffentlichungen/Working_Paper/ WP_2011-01.pdf.

Gartner. 2017. "Worldwide Sales of Smartphones 2016." 2017. https://www. gartner.com/newsroom/id/3609817.

Gartzke, Erik, and Yonatan Lupu. 2012. "Trading on Preconceptions: Why World War I Was Not a Failure of Economic Interdependence." *International Security* 36 (4): 115–50.

General Administration of Customs of the People's Republic of China. 2018. "Imports and Exports by Customs Regime, 7.2018." Monthly Statistics Bulletin. 2018. http://english.customs.gov.cn/Statics/bebb13fd-8843-4e0e-a6ce-04078af05 648.html.

General Motors. 2016. "General Motors Announces Growth Strategy for China." 2016. http://media.gm.com/media/cn/en/gm/news.detail.html/content/Pages/news/cn/en/2016/Mar/0321_annoucement.html.

— 2017. "2016 Full-Year and Fourth-Quarter Earnings." http://media.gm.com/content/dam/Media/gmcom/investor/2017/feb/earnings/GeneralMotors-q4-2016-Earnings.pdf.

Glosserman, Brad. 2013. "A 'New Type of Great Power Relations'? Hardly." 40. PacNet. Honolulu.

Goldman Sachs Global Investment Research. 2015. "20 S&P 500 Stocks with the Highest Sales Exposure to China Based on 2014 Company Fillings." https://qz.com/853032/these-are-the-us-companies-and-states-that-will-suffer-most-if-us-china-relations-worsen/.

Gosen, Bradley Van, Philip L. Verplanck, and Poul Emsbo. 2019. "Rare Earth Element Mineral Deposits in the United States." Reston (Virginia).

Governments of Canada / United States / Mexico. 2012. *North American Free Trade Agreement.* http://www.naftanow.org/agreement/default_en.asp.

Heilmann, Kilian. 2016. "Does Political Conflict Hurt Trade? Evidence from Consumer Boycotts." *Journal of International Economics* 99: 179–91. https://doi.org/10.1016/j.jinteco.2015.11.008.

Hewlett Packard. 2017. "Hewlett Packard Supplier List." http://h20195.www2.hp.com/v2/getpdf.aspx/c03728062.pdf.

Hirschman, Albert. O. 1977. *The Passions and the Interests: Political Arguments for Capitalism Before Its Triumph.* Princeton: Princeton University Press. https://doi.org/10.2307/j.ctt3fgz1q.

Hong Kong Trade and Industry Department. 2017. "Hong Kong's Re-Exports by Main Origin." Key Statistics of Hong Kong External Merchandise Trade. 2017. https://www.tid.gov.hk/english/aboutus/publications/tradestat/rxori.html.

Howse, Robert. 2006. "Montesquieu on Commerce, Conquest, War, and Peace." *Brooklyn Journal of International Law* 31: 1–16. http://heinonlinebackup.com/hol-cgi-bin/get_pdf.cgi?handle=hein.journals/bjil31&section=30%5Cnhttp://www.law.nyu.edu/ecm_dlv1/groups/public/@nyu_law_website__faculty__faculty_profiles__rhowse/documents/ecm_pro_060042.pdf.

Huang, Ji kun, Wei Wei, Qi Cui, and Wei Xie. 2017. "The Prospects for China's Food Security and Imports: Will China Starve the World via Imports?" *Journal of Integrative Agriculture* 16 (12): 2933–44. https://doi.org/10.1016/S2095-3119(17)61756-8.

Hurt, Chris, Wallace E. Tyner, and Farzad Taheripour. 2018. "Chinese Tariffs on Soybeans and Pork: U.S. and Indiana Impacts." April 2018. Purdue Agricultural Economics Report.

iFixit. 2017a. "IPhone 8 Teardown." 2017. https://www.ifixit.com/Teardown/iPhone+8+Teardown/97481.

— 2017b. "IPhone X Teardown." 2017. https://www.ifixit.com/Teardown/iPhone+X+Teardown/98975.

Ikenberry, G. John. 2008. "The Rise of China and the Future of the West." *Foreign Affairs* 87 (1): 23–37. https://doi.org/10.2307/20020265.

International Trade Administration. 2017. "China - Medical Devices - Leading Sectors for US Exports and Investments." 2017. https://www.export.gov/article?id=China-Medical-Devices.

International Trade Center. 2018. "Trade Map - Trade Statistics for International Business Development." 2018. https://www.trademap.org/(X(1)S(upem1b55wke 4ea31fb5ykm45))/Index.aspx.

Jervis, Robert. 1978. "Cooperation Under the Security Dilemma." *World Politics* 30 (2): 167–214.

Johnson, Robert C., and Guillermo Noguera. 2012. "Accounting for Intermediates: Production Sharing and Trade in Value Added." *Journal of International Economics* 86 (2): 224–36. https://doi.org/10.1016/j.jinteco.2011.10.003.

Kakeas, Konstantin. 2016. "The All-American IPhone." *MIT Technology Review*, 2016. https://www.technologyreview.com/s/601491/the-all-american-iphone/.

Kant, Immanuel. 1795. *Zum Ewigen Frieden: Ein Philosophischer Entwurf.* Edited by Rudolf Malter. Stuttgart: Philipp Reclam jun. GmbH & Co. KG.

Keohane, Robert O. 2002. "Introduction: From Interdependence and Institutions to Globalization and Governance." In *Power and Governance in a Partially Globalized World*, edited by Robert O. Keohane, 1st ed., 312. London: Routledge.

Keohane, Robert O., and Joseph S. Nye. 1989. *Power and Interdependence.* 2nd ed. New York: Longman.

Kissinger, Henry. 2011. *On China.* New York: Penguin Press.

— 2014. *World Order.* New York: Penguin Press.

Langer, Lissy, Daniel Huppmann, and Franziska Holz. 2016. "Lifting the US Crude Oil Export Ban: A Numerical Partial Equilibrium Analysis." *Energy Policy* 97: 258–66. https://doi.org/10.1016/j.enpol.2016.07.040.

Lardy, Nicholas R. 2006. "China: Toward a Consumption-Driven Growth Path." *Policy Briefs in International Economics, Institute for International Economics*, 2006.

Lawrence, Robert Z. 2018. "Five Reasons Why the Focus on Trade Deficits Is Misleading." 18–6. https://piie.com/publications/policy-briefs/five-reasons-why-focus-trade-deficits-misleading.

Lenin, Vladimir Ilyich. 1970. *Imperialism, the Highest Stage of Capitalism.* New York: International Publishers.

Lenovo. 2018. "2017/2018 Annual Report." https://doc.irasia.com/listco/hk/lenovo/annual/2018/ar2018.pdf.

Li, Quan, and Rafael Reuveny. 2008. "Trading for Peace? Disaggregated Bilateral Trade and Interstate Military Conflict Initiation." *Journal of Peace Research*, no. 812: 1–41.

Lieberthal, Kenneth, and Wang Jisi. 2012. "Addressing US-China Strategic Distrust." *John L. Thronton China Center At Brookings Monograph Series* 4 (March): 1–50. http://yahuwshua.org/en/Resource-584/0330_china_lieberthal.pdf.

Lovely, Mary E, and Yang Liang. 2018. "Trump Tariffs Primarily Hit Multinational Supply Chains, Harm US Technology Competitiveness." https://piie.com/system/files/documents/pb18-12.pdf.

Mansfield, Edward D., and Brian M. Pollins. 2001. "The Study of Interdependence and Conflict: Recent Advances, Open Questions, and Directions for Future Research." *Journal of Conflict Resolution* 45 (6): 834–59. https://doi.org/10.1177/0022002701045006007.

Mauro, Filippo di, Stephane Dees, and Warwick J. McKibbin. 2008. "International Linkages in the Context of Global and Regional Integration." In *Globalisation, Regionlism and Economic Interdependence*, edited by Filippo di Mauro, Stephane Dees, and Warwick J. McKibbin. Cambridge: Cambridge University Press.

McKinsey. 2017. "The Medtech Opportunity for Japanese Companies." Industry Analysis. 2017. https://www.mckinsey.com/industries/pharmaceuticals-and-medical-products/our-insights/the-medtech-opportunity-for-japanese-companies.

McMillan, Susan M. 1997. "Interdependence and Conflict." *Mershon International Studies Review* 41 (1): 33–58. https://doi.org/10.2307/222802.

Mearsheimer, J. J. 2001. *The Tragedy of Great Power Politics*. New York: Norton.

— 2010. "The Gathering Storm: China's Challenge to US Power in Asia." *The Chinese Journal of International Politics* 3 (4): 381–96. https://doi.org/10.1093/cjip/poq016.

Morrison, Wayne M. 2018. "China-U.S. Trade Issues." *Congressional Research Service*.

National Bureau of Statistics of China. 2019. "Statistical Communiqué of the People's Republic of China on the 2018 National Economic and Social Development." 2019. http://www.stats.gov.cn/english/PressRelease/201902/t20190228_1651335.html.

New York Times. 2012. "Anti-Japanese Protests Over Disputed Islands Continue in China." New York Times. 2012. https://www.nytimes.com/2012/09/17/world/asia/anti-japanese-protests-over-disputed-islands-continue-in-china.html.

Ng Eng Hen. 2019. "Shangri-La Dialogue: Shifting Economic Dependencies Could Lead to Parallel Blocs." The Strait Times. 2019. https://www.straitstimes.com/singapore/shangri-la-dialogue-shifting-economic-dependencies-could-lead-to-parallel-blocs-says-ng.

Nie, Jun, and Andrew Palmer. 2016. "Consumer Spending in China: The Past and the Future." *Economic Review* 101 (3): 25–49.

OECD, and WTO. 2012. "Trade in Value Added: Concepts, Methodologies and Challenges (Joint OECD-WTO Note)" 2010 (October 2010): 28. www.oecd.org/sti/ind/49894138.pdf.

— 2015a. "Trade in Value Added - China." https://www.oecd.org/sti/ind/tiva/CN_2015_China.pdf.

— 2015b. "Trade in Value Added - United States." https://www.oecd.org/sti/ind/tiva/CN_2015_UnitedStates.pdf.

Oneal, John R., and Bruce M. Russet. 1997. "The Classical Liberals Were Right: Democracy, Interdependence, and Conflict, 1950-1985." *International Studies Quarterly* 41 (2): 267–94. https://doi.org/10.1111/1468-2478.00042.

Oneal, John R., Bruce Russett, and Michael L. Berbaum. 2003. "Causes of Peace: Democracy, Interdependence, and International Organizations, 1885-1992."

International Studies Quarterly 47 (3): 371–93. https://doi.org/10.1111/1468-2478.4703004.

Organski, A.F.K. 1968. *World Politics*. 2nd Editio. New York: Knopf.

Organski, A.F.K., and Jacek Kugler. 1980. *The War Ledger*. Chicago: University of Chicago Press.

Oxford Economics. 2017. "Understanding the US- China Trade Relation." https://www.uschina.org/sites/default/files/Oxford Economics US Jobs and China Trade Report.pdf.

Papayoanou, Paul, and Scott L. Kastner. 2000. "Sleeping with the (Potential) Enemy – Assessing the U.S. Policy of Engagement with China." In *Power and the Purse – Economic Statecraft, Interdependence and National Secuirty*, edited by Jean-Marc F. Blanchard, Edward D. Mansfield, and Norrin M. Ripsman. London: Frank Lass.

Paulson, Henry M. 2019. "Remarks by Henry M. Paulson, Jr., on the Risks of an 'Economic Iron Curtain.'" Paulson Institute. 2019. http://www.paulsoninstitute.org/news/2019/02/27/remarks-by-henry-m-paulson-jr-on-the-risks-of-an-economic-iron-curtain/.

ProClinical. 2018. "The Top 10 Medical Device Companies 2018." 2018. https://www.proclinical.com/blogs/2018-5/the-top-10-medical-device-companies-2018.

PwC. 2017. "Global Top 100 Companies by Market Capitalisation," no. June: 1–35. https://www.pwc.com/gx/en/audit-services/assets/pdf/global-top-100-companies-2017-final.pdf.

Qualcomm. 2015. "Qualcomm and ZTE Sign New 3G/4G License, Strengthening Long-Term Partnership | Qualcomm." Press Release. 2015. https://www.qualcomm.com/news/releases/2015/11/02/qualcomm-and-zte-sign-new-3g4g-license-strengthening-long-term-partnership.

— 2017. "Annual Report 2017." http://investor.qualcomm.com/annuals-proxies.cfm.

Quanta Computer. 2018. "Company Introduction - Factory Overview." 2018. http://www.quantacn.com/EnWeb/CompanyProfile.aspx.

Quartz. 2018a. "A New US-ZTE Deal Will Keep China's Smartphone Giant Alive." 2018. https://qz.com/1299684/a-new-us-zte-deal-will-keep-chinas-smartphone-giant-alive/.

— 2018b. "The Hottest Stock in the S&P Is AMD." 2018. https://qz.com/1371383/the-hottest-stock-in-the-sp-is-a-nearly-50-year-old-chip-maker/.

— 2018c. "Why the Semiconductor Is Suddenly at the Heart of US-China Tech Tensions." 2018. https://qz.com/1335801/us-china-tech-why-the-semiconductor-is-suddenly-at-the-heart-of-us-china-tensions/.

Reuveny, Rafael, and Heejoon Kang. 1998. "Bilateral Trade and Political Conflict/Cooperation: Do Goods Matter?" *Journal of Peace Research* 35 (5): 581–602.

Ripsman, Norrin M., and Jean-Marc F. Blanchard. 2003. "Qualitative Research on Economic Interdependence and Conflict: Overcoming Methodological Hurdles." In *Economic Interdependence and International Conflict*, edited by Edward D. Mansfield and Brian M. Pollins, 310–23. Ann Arbour: The University of Michigan Press.

Rosecrance, Richard. 2013. "The Rise of the Trading State: Commerce and Conquest in the Modern World." In *Conflict after the Cold War: Arguments on Causes of War and Peace*, edited by Richard K. Betts. Boston: Pearson.

SEMI. 2017. "The Rise of China IC Industry - As A Global Ecosystem Partner." Shanghai. http://www.semi.org/en/sites/semi.org/files/data17/docs/The Rise of China IC Industry - As a Global Ecosystem Partner.pdf.

Semiconductor Industry Association. 2018. "U.S. Semiconductor Industry Impact." 2018. https://www.semiconductors.org/semiconductors-101/industry-impact/.

Skyworks. 2016. "2016 Annual Report." http://cms.ipressroom.com.s3.amazonaws.com/249/files/20177/HA+Annual+Report+2016.pdf.

— 2018a. "Corporate Overview." http://www.skyworksinc.com/downloads/about/skyworks_overview.pdf.

— 2018b. "Skyworks Facility Locations." 2018. http://www.skyworksinc.com/AboutLocations.aspx.

Stewart, Michael. 1984. *The Age of Interdependence: Economic Policy in a Shrinking World*. Cambridge, Mass.: MIT Press.

Swanson, Ana, and Alexandra Stevensen. 2018. "Qualcomm May Be Collateral Damage in a U.S.-China Trade War." *New York Times*, April 2018. https://www.nytimes.com/2018/04/18/us/politics/qualcomm-us-china-trade-war.html?rref=collection%2Ftimestopic%2FQualcomm Inc.

Tammen, Ronald, Jacek Kugler, and Douglas Lemke. 2000. *Power Transitions: Strategies for the 21st Century*. New York: Chatham House.

The Economist. 2009. "Saying Originally Attributed to John Maynard Keynes and Used by Chinese Top Economist." Quote of the Day. 2009. https://www.economist.com/free-exchange/2009/04/13/quote-of-the-day.

— 2017. "Donald Trump and Xi Jinping Are Not so Friendly after All - The End of the Beginning." 2017. https://www.economist.com/china/2017/07/08/donald-trump-and-xi-jinping-are-not-so-friendly-after-all.

— 2018. "An American Ban Puts China's ZTE in Peril - Not so Phoney War." *The Economist, Print Edition, April 21st 2018*, 2018. https://www.economist.com/business/2018/04/21/an-american-ban-puts-chinas-zte-in-peril.

— 2019a. "Corporate America Is Growing More Dissatisfied with Donald Trump." 2019. https://www.economist.com/graphic-detail/2019/06/26/corporate-america-is-growing-more-dissatisfied-with-donald-trump.

— 2019b. "Does Apple's Boss Have a Plan B in China? - Schumpeter." *The Economist, Print Edition, May 30th*, 2019. https://www.economist.com/business/2019/05/30/does-apples-boss-have-a-plan-b-in-china.

— 2019c. "Why You Should Never Start a Trade War with an Autocracy." 2019. https://www.economist.com/graphic-detail/2019/04/27/why-you-should-never-start-a-trade-war-with-an-autocracy.

The People's Bank of China. 2005. "China Monetary Report, Quarter Two, 2005." Beijing.

The World Bank. 2016. "Households and NPISHs Final Consumption Expenditure (Current US$)." 2016. https://data.worldbank.org/indicator/NE.CON.PRVT.CD?end=2016&start=1960&year_high_desc=true.

— 2017. "Gross Domestic Product 2016." *World Development Indicators Database*, no. April: 1–5. http://databank.worldbank.org/data/download/GDP.pdf.

—— 2018a. "China - Annual GDP Growth in %." 2018. https://data.worldbank.org/indicator/NY.GDP.MKTP.KD.ZG?end=2017&locations=CN&start=1989.

—— 2018b. "Exports of Goods and Services (% of GDP), China." 2018. https://doi.org/10.1787/0fe445d9-en.

TrendForce. 2018. "Global Laptop Market from 2016 to 2018." https://press.trendforce.com/press/20180212-3065.html.

Trump, Donald. 2014. "Twitter Quote on Global Trade Deficit (Numbers from United States Census Bureau)." Twitter. 2014. https://twitter.com/realDonaldTrump/status/474213293717200897.

—— 2015. *Crippled America: How to Make America Great Again.* New York: Simon and Schuster.

—— 2017. "Twitter Quote on China (One-Sided Trade)." Twitter. 2017. https://twitter.com/realdonaldtrump/status/816068355555815424.

—— 2018a. "Twitter Quote on China ($500 Billion Trade Deficit)." Twitter. 2018. https://twitter.com/realdonaldtrump/status/981492087328792577.

—— 2018b. "Twitter Quote on China (Trade Wars Are Easy to Win)." 2018. https://twitter.com/realdonaldtrump/status/969525362580484098?lang=de.

—— 2019. "Quote on China (We Will Make a Deal with China)." 2019. https://twitter.com/realdonaldtrump/status/1128257891805298690.

U.S. Department of Commerce. 2017. "Top U.S. Trading Partner Ranked by 2017 U.S. Total Export Value of Goods." 2017. https://www.trade.gov/mas/ian/build/groups/public/@tg_ian/documents/webcontent/tg_ian_003364.pdf.

—— 2018. "Commerce Department Lifts Ban After ZTE Deposits Final Tranche of $1.4 Billion Penalty | Department of Commerce." Press Release. 2018. https://www.commerce.gov/news/press-releases/2018/07/commerce-department-lifts-ban-after-zte-deposits-final-tranche-14.

U.S. Department of the Treasury. 2018a. "Foreign Holdings of U.S. Securities as of June 30, 2017." http://ticdata.treasury.gov/Publish/shla2017r.pdf.

—— 2018b. "Major Foreign Holders of Treasury Securities." Washington, D.C. https://ticdata.treasury.gov/Publish/mfh.txt.

U.S. Geological Survey. 2019. "Rare Earths Statistics and Information." Reston (Virginia). https://prd-wret.s3-us-west-2.amazonaws.com/assets/palladium/production/atoms/files/mcs-2019-raree.pdf.

Uchitell, Louis. 1989. "Spread of U.S. Plants Abroad Is Slowing Exports." *New York Times*, 1989. https://www.nytimes.com/1989/03/26/us/spread-of-us-plants-abroad-is-slowing-exports.html.

UN Comtrade. 2018. "UN Comtrade | International Trade Statistics Database." 2018. http://comtrade.un.org/.

UN Trade Statistics. 1998. *INTERNATIONAL MERCHANDISE TRADE STATISTICS : Concepts and Definitions.* https://doi.org/10.1007/s13398-014-0173-7.2.

—— 2015. "Bilateral Trade Asymmetries." http://unstats.un.org/unsd/tradekb/Attachment407.aspx?AttachmentType=1.

—— 2016. "United Nations International Trade Statistics Database [Online]." 2016. https://unstats.un.org/unsd/tradekb/Knowledgebase/50075/What-is-UN-Comtrade.

United Magnetics. 2019a. "Applications for Rare Earth Permanent Magnets." 2019. http://www.umag.com.cn/index.php?m=&c=Index&a=lists&catid=3.

— 2019b. "The Permanent Magnets Have Been Removed from the US New Tariff List - United Magnetics Co., Ltd." 2019. http://www.umag.com.cn/index. php?m=&c=Index&a=show&catid=32&id=110.

United States Census Bureau. 2019. "Trade in Goods with China." U.S. Export and Import Statistics. 2019. https://www.census.gov/foreign-trade/balance/c5700. html.

US & China Statistics Working Group. 2012. "The Second Phase Report on the Statistical Discrepancy of Merchandise Trade between the United States and China." http://www.esa.doc.gov/sites/default/files/2ndphasereportjcctsigned1. pdf.

US House of Representatives. 2018. "Statement of John Heisdorffer President, American Soybean Association before the Committee on Ways and Means, U.S. House of Representatives." https://waysandmeans.house.gov/wp-content/ uploads/2018/04/20180412-Testimony-John-Heisdorffer-Testimony.pdf.

Waltz, Kenneth N. 2013. "Theory of International Politics." In *Conflict after the Cold War: Arguments on Causes of War and Peace*, edited by Richard K. Betts. Boston: Pearson.

Weber, Max. 1949. *The Methodology of Social Sciences*. Edited by Edward A. Shils and Henry A. Finch. Glencoe: The Free Press of Glencoe.

White, Hugh, Chen Weihua, and Wu Jianmin. 2014. "A New Type of Great Power Dialogue?" Foreign Policy. 2014. http://foreignpolicy.com/2014/11/03/a-new-type-of-great-power-dialogue/.

World Customs Organization. 2018. "Nomenclature and Classification of Goods." 2018. http://www.wcoomd.org/en/topics/nomenclature/overview.aspx.

Xing, Yuqing. 2014. "China's High Tech Exports: The Myth and Reality." *Asian Economic Papers* 13 (1): 110–23.

Xing, Yuqing, and Neal Detert. 2010. "How the IPhone Widens the United States Trade Deficit with the People's Republic of China." ADBI Working Paper. Tokyo.

Xinhua News Agency. 2017. "China Focus: Construction of Boeing's First Overseas 737 Factory Starts in China o Title." http://www.xinhuanet.com/english/2017-05/11/c_136274218.htm.

— 2018. "Truth behind China-U.S. 'Trade Imbalances.'" 2018. http://www. xinhuanet.com/english/2018-03/27/c_137069649.htm.

Yang, Dali L. 1991. "China Adjusts to the World Economy: The Political Economy of China's Coastal Development Strategy." *Pacific Affairs* 64 (1): 42–64.

Yang, Hongxing, and Dingxin Zhao. 2015. "Performance Legitimacy, State Autonomy and China's Economic Miracle." *Journal of Contemporary China* 24 (91): 64–82. https://doi.org/10.1080/10670564.2014.918403.

Yao, Yang. 2011. "The Relationship between China's Export-Led Growth and Its Double Transition of Demographic Change and Industrialization." *Asian Economic Papers* 10 (2): 52–76.

Zhang, Zhiwei, and Yi Xiong. 2018. "China Macro: US Economic Balances with Partners." Deutsche Bank Research. 2018. https://www.dbresearch.com/servlet/ reweb2.ReWEB?rwnode=RPS_EN-PROD$PROD0000000000464258&rwsite= RPS_EN-PROD&rwobj=ReDisplay.Start.class&document=PROD0000000000 470470.

Zhu, Andong, and David M. Kotz. 2011. "The Dependence of China's Economic Growth on Exports and Investments." *Review of Radical Political Economics* 43 (1): 9–32. https://doi.org/10.1177/0486613410383951.

Zhu, Yuchao. 2011. "'Performance Legitimacy' and China's Political Adaptation Strategy." *Journal of Chinese Political Science* 16 (2): 123–40. https://doi.org/10.1007/s11366-011-9140-8.

Zoellick, Robert. 2005. "„Whither China: From Membership to Responsibility?", Remarks to National Committee on U.S.-China Relations." New York. http://2001-2009.state.gov/s/d/former/zoellick/rem/53682.htm.

9 Index

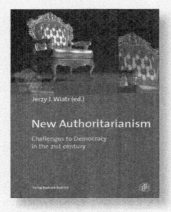

Andreea Zamfira | Christian de Montlibert | Daniela Radu (eds.)

Gender in Focus: Identities, Codes, Stereotypes and Politics

2018 • 370 pp. • Pb. • 49,90 € (D) • 51,30 € (A)
ISBN 978-3-8474-2183-2 • eISBN 978-3-8474-1211-3

This book deals with the interplay between identities, codes, stereotypes and politics governing the various constructions and deconstructions of gender in several Western and non-Western societies (Germany, Italy, Serbia, Romania, Cameroon, Indonesia, Vietnam, and others). Readers are invited to discover the realm of gender studies and to reflect upon the transformative potentialities of globalisation and interculturality.

The Editors:

Dr. Andreea Zamfira, Assistant Professor, Lucian Blaga University of Sibiu, Romania | Dr. Christian de Montlibert, Emeritus Professor, University Marc Bloch, Strasbourg, France | Dr. Daniela Radu, Independent Researcher

www.barbara-budrich.net

Marianne Kneuer
Helen V. Milner (eds.)

Political Science and Digitalization – Global Perspectives

2019 · 290 pp. · Hardcover · 60,00 € (D) · US$85.00, GBP 53.00
ISBN 978-3-8474-2332-4 · eISBN 978-3-8474-1488-9

Digitalization is not only a new research subject for political science, but a transformative force for the discipline in terms of teaching and learning as well as research methods and publishing. This volume provides the first account of the influence of digitalization on the discipline of political science including contributions from 20 different countries. It presents a regional stocktaking of the challenges and opportunities of digitalization in most world regions.

Marianne Kneuer is Professor for Political Science and Director of the Institute of Social Sciences and Co-founder of the Center for digital Change at the University of Hildesheim, Germany.

Helen V. Milner is B.C. Forbes Professor of Politics and International Affairs at Princeton University as well as Director of the Niehaus Center for Globalization and Governance at Princeton's Woodrow Wilson School, USA.

www.barbara-budrich.net

Marianne Kristiansen

Jørgen Bloch-Poulsen

Action Research in Organizations

Participation in Change Processes

2021. 328 pp. • Pb. • 39,90 € (D) • 41,10 € (A)
ISBN 978-3-8474-2377-5 • eISBN 978-3-8474-1663-0

Who decides to initiate change processes in organizations? Who sets the goals? What does it mean for employees to participate in change processes? The book examines organizational change processes based on collaboration between employers, employees and action researchers in Europe and the U.S. in the later part of the 20th century. The authors offer important insights into participation and change in organizations for researchers and practitioners by identifying dilemmas and paradoxes, conflicting interests and exercising of power.

www.shop.budrich.de

Pamela M. Barnes | Ian G. Barnes

The Politics of Nucelar Energy in the European Union

Framing the Discourse: Actors, Positions and Dynamics

For the foreseeable future the overall use of nuclear electricity in the European Union is unlikely to change significantly despite the controversies surrounding its use amongst the EU's nation states. The author questions the role that nuclear electricity plays in meeting the challenges of providing secure, competitive and sustainable energy to support the development of the low carbon economy in the EU.

2018 • 292 pp. • Pb.
58,00 € (D) • 59,70 € (A)
ISBN 978-3-8474-0687-7
eISBN 978-3-8474-0831-4

Maria Marczewska-Rytko (ed.)

Handbook of Direct Democracy in Central and Eastern Europe after 1989

Since the collapse of the Soviet Union the political history of Central and Eastern Europe has been mainly the story of arise, consolidation, transformation and struggles of new democratic regimes and societies. This handbook offers an instructive approach to that history focusing on the relevance of practices and institutions of direct democracy.

2018 • 351 pp. • Pb.
64,90 € (D) • 66,80 € (A)
ISBN 978-3-8474-2122-1
eISBN 978-3-8474-1110-9

www.barbara-budrich.net

US-China tensions over global supremacy escalated over the last years, increasing the likelihood of a future conflict. However, open conflict would have costly consequences for both sides due to the countries' deep economic interconnectedness. Against this backdrop, the book addresses the question how high the incentives for both sides are to avoid conflict and continue cooperation out of economic considerations.

The author:
Dr. rer. pol. Frank Mouritz is a Research Fellow at the Bundeswehr University Munich and Academic Coordinator at the George C. Marshall European Center for Security Studies, Garmisch-Partenkirchen, Germany.

ISBN 978-3-8474-2516-8

9 783847 425168

www.budrich.eu